Muire O' Connell

Diary of a
Student Social Worker

By the same author

Diary of a Delinquent Episode

Diary of a Student Social Worker

Jane Sparrow

Routledge & Kegan Paul
London, Henley and Boston

First published in 1978
by Routledge & Kegan Paul Ltd
39 Store Street,
London WC1E 7DD,
Broadway House,
Newtown Road,
Henley-on-Thames,
Oxon RG9 1EN and
9 Park Street,
Boston, Mass. 02108, USA
Set in 11 on 12 pt Plantin by
Kelly & Wright, Bradford-on-Avon, Wiltshire
and printed in Great Britain by
Lowe & Brydone Printers Ltd
Thetford, Norfolk

British Library Cataloguing in Publication Data

Sparrow, Jane
Diary of a student social worker
1. Social work with children – England
I. Title
362.7'092'4   HV751.A6   77–30664
ISBN 0 7100 8857 4

Contents

People and situations

Marlshire County Children's Department
Mr Tasker: county children's officer
Miss Farrar: deputy children's officer, and student supervisor
Miss Gibbs: east area children's officer
Fieldstaff: Miss Beckwith, Mrs Garvey, Mrs Marren, Mr Ripley
Brayley Children's Home: Mr and Mrs Coombs (in charge)
Redlands reception centre: Mr and Mrs Willcox (in charge)
Other foster-parents: Mr and Mrs Dell, Mr and Mrs Watson, Mr and Mrs Chapel and others
Administrative staff: Mrs Burke, Mr Hebditch (court officer), Mr Parfit and others
Committee members: Lord Brackendale, Mr Browne, Mrs ffrench, Captain Shaw-Cooper, Mrs Armstrong and others
Other children's departments: Marlford City, Cameronshire, Hassex, Loamshire, East Dowling, Germany
Workers in other agencies: Inspector Worth, NSPCC
Miss Young, Miss Onslow (psychiatric social workers)
Miss Grainger (educational psychologist)
Mental welfare officer, probation officers, health visitors, education welfare officers, general practitioners, school teachers

Father O'Sullivan (Roman Catholic priest)

Mrs Merrill (organizer, Marlford Adoption Society)

Student's Work

A Applications for reception into care

1 Mrs Chubb, mother of Linda (aged 5), Susan (4), and Tracey (2½) pp. 6, 8–9, 12–15, 16–18, 22, 30–continued later

2 Mr and Mrs Rock, parents of Jenny (aged 4) pp. 24–9, 45, 114, 131

3 Mr and Mrs Hopgood, parents of Keith (aged 6), Sam (4½) and Karen (14 months) pp. 54–5, 58–9, 60–1, 62–5, 66–7, 76, 80, 82, 83, 90, 91, 92, 96–7, 101–4, 112–13, 122–4, 137, 144

B Three long-term foster-homes

4 Mrs Almond, with Eamon Murphy (aged 12; mother Miss Kathleen Murphy) pp. 10–11, 18–20, 23, 29–31, 32–7, 42, 43–4, 45, 47–8, 49–50, 57, 71–4, 78–9, 97–8, 106–7, 111, 122, 127–8, 137–41, 144

5 Mr and Mrs Yates, with George Gardiner (aged 13) and Jimmy Best (aged 10); mothers Miss Gardiner, Miss Best pp. 20–1, 32, 36, 37–8, 42, 45, 47, 61, 85, 121, 132–3, 143

6 Mr and Mrs Bateson, with David (aged 11, adopted) and Sally (5) pp. 22, 45, 50, 71, 143

C Selection of foster-parents

7 Mr and Mrs Tolley (later fostered Carol, aged 12) pp. 38–42, 45, 53–4, 58, 67–8, 69–71, 74–5, 76, 82–3, 84, 85, 87–90, 106, 126–7

8 Mrs Nash (great-aunt to Yvonne, aged 13, from London) pp. 69, 80, 110, 113–14, 136–7, 142, 144

D Adoption welfare supervision

9 Mr and Mrs Hicks, with Carmen placed for adoption (2½ months old) and their own son Leslie (aged 10) pp. 46, 54, 79, 104–5, 126, 135–6

E Guardian ad litem
10 Mr and Mrs Stokes, adopting her daughter Frances (aged 10) pp. 46, 55, 57–8, 78, 122

F Selection of adopters
11 Mr and Mrs Pizzy (second placement) pp. 79–80

G Enquiries family casework
12 Mr and Mrs McTavish from Cameronshire (four children of two marriages) pp. 46, 52–3, 55, 56, 65, 77, 78, 86–7, 92, 111–12

13 Gregory (aged 16) and Joe (aged 12)—two coloured boys boarded-out with Mrs Victor; mothers Mrs White, and Mrs Kemp pp. 46, 61–2, 65, 68, 71, 78, 81–2, 83–4, 93–6, 111, 115–19, 124–6, 131–2, 142–3

14 Erika (aged 10) daughter of Mrs Strickland from Germany, with Mr Strickland and their children Rosa ($3\frac{1}{2}$) and Richard (2 months) pp. 98–101, 112, 113, 114–15, 122, 142

H Place of Safety Orders
15 Chubb family continued (Linda, Susan, Tracey, and the baby, Jayne) pp. 60, 87, 92, 107–10, 111, 113, 115, 129–30, 133–5, 142

Introduction

Until recently, having published my *Diary of a Delinquent Episode*, it did not occur to me to write a sequel. However, one thing tends to lead to another, so this second *Diary of a Student Social Worker* has now emerged. Both were written a long time ago, within two years of each other, and have (especially the second) needed little alteration except for a complete change of names—so all names of people and places are fictitious. The changed names together with a considerable time-lapse should, hopefully, offend nobody. Indeed, this second diary (as opposed to the first) contains relatively little risking offence—rather the reverse.

The first diary was written of my own volition, except in so far as I was inwardly driven, towards the end of my five-year period of residential work in a farm-centred institution for adolescent girls. This sequel, except that I enjoyed writing behind the scenes, was required of me as a student during the final five months of a training course for professional social work. The first diary was drastically pruned for publication; the second appears now in its original form. Unlike the first, this is a real diary, written day by day over a comparatively short period. Whereas the first was more an overview constructed with a certain amount of close hindsight while still on the premises, this second record never knew quite what might happen tomorrow. Through being written just as it happened, it is more 'accurate' in one sense, but again otherwise merely describes one person's subjective experience. Naturally, it was my private version of events; my parallel records for the purposes of supervision and swelling the department's files were somewhat different and more formal.

During my two-year postgraduate course (while training as a 'mature' student in between my first and second jobs) we had several fieldwork placements, either for block periods or running concurrently with academic work in the university. My placements included a stretch as a nurse in a psychiatric hospital together with experience alongside the hospital's psychiatric social workers; a spring and summer in a voluntary agency catering for families and individuals of all ages with a wide range of problems, and several months' attachment to a child guidance clinic. This diary covers the final placement (we simply submitted a résumé of former practical work) in the Marlshire County Children's Department. The placement started on 21 March and continued for three days each week (with the other two days in the university) until our exams towards the end of May; from mid-June until late August the placement was full-time.

The first diary was originally written with a view to future understanding of 'a confusing, often frightening experience', and later published because of concern for people in all forms of residential care, and concern for their care-givers who have special need of support in such demanding work. It is less easy to say why this second diary is being published now—perhaps partly because it depicts a former residential worker during professional training for field social work. Traditionally and unfortunately, there is some tension and mutual suspicion between the two types of social worker (residential staff and fieldworkers), partially in rivalship terms of which carries the tougher, more essential role. In reality both tasks can be equally difficult, though the typical pressures of each are different.

It must be confessed that, whilst a residential worker, I regarded the few probation officers and child care officers I met as fairly weak creatures who evaded the daily sweat of living alongside explosive clients. Since then I know at first hand the pressures of fieldwork, particularly in that a non-residential worker by definition has not the security of a consistent roof over her head and may search desperately for a bed anywhere by nightfall for homeless clients. Readers may decide there is little to choose between the stress for Redlands staff (coping twenty-four hours a day with young Keith and Sam plus nearly twenty more unsettled children and adolescents) and the stress of the fieldworker trying to make plans, travelling long distances between all parties, searching in a vacuum for the mother who deserted Keith and Sam.

Another possible reason for publication is a slight 'historical interest'. Although no date for the year is given, the work described is evidently before the Children and Young Persons Act 1963, at a time when children's departments were well established, though as variable nationally then as today, with some (such as Loamshire) already anticipating the Act by undertaking preventive work with families in an extra effort to maintain children in their own homes. Marlshire, without committing itself to much preventive work, was properly confident of its high standards in carrying out statutory responsibilities. Social workers today, often Jacks-of-all-trades in much larger multi-purpose organizations, may react enviously or impatiently in thinking of the former Marlshire children's department when it was so clear-cut and circumscribed in its policy.

If latter-day fieldstaff protest that it would be impossible now to afford the same amount of time and energy for children at risk and their parent-figures, we may question whether our new, vast 'generic' social services departments are an improvement upon their precursors. On the other hand, it could be argued that the sheer volume and variety of work today (on behalf of a wide range of people of all ages referred to one big agency) tends to reduce an element of nosey-parkering interference which may sometimes have featured in the past. Apparently today, there is less time for busy-bodies to make mischief, though there may be more scope for idle fingers to twiddle during frequent agency meetings and in chatting with one's team while complaining that there is no time to deal with a mountain of work. Another contrast is that this diary describes a rural county dotted with small towns and outlying villages, which entails more travelling time with scope for thought and relaxation between interviews, whereas many fieldworkers prefer confinement within large cities and cannot easily believe in the similar (even more earthy sometimes) nature of problems in rural areas where stark distress appears to be offset by a family's possession of an apple-tree in their garden.

A third justification for making this diary available is that it may possibly inform the general public about a few of the situations in which we become involved, and what we feel about it. Social workers currently hit the newspaper headlines in a way which used not to happen; they do not enjoy much popularity at present, and perhaps never will, being contaminated in the eyes of some unwilling spectators through their involvement in alarming or disgraceful situations. Indeed, it almost seems as though 'society', having strained itself towards slightly greater tolerance of the recipients of the social services, is now hypercritical of its own representatives who mediate between it and its less fortunate members. It is time the public realized that social workers are ordinary human beings, with specialized knowledge and skills but without magic wands.

However, it would be foolish to imagine that this student-diary gives a typical account of the modern workload of a social services department employee. If the reader first thinks of a number of 'cases' allocated to a student as described in these pages, he should then multiply that number at least five times, possibly ten times, in order to gain an impression of ordinary employment, and add a much greater range of situations even as applied simply to children, plus responsibilities for physically and mentally ill and handicapped adults and the elderly; then add and multiply again for good measure since the reorganization of services and local authority boundaries, and subtract nothing—so he will certainly not finish with the number he first thought of. (Even so, it is still, and always was, only possible to do a day's work within a day under whatever conditions, so perhaps the difference now is not that social services employees work harder but that they work under greater pressure both of numbers and of anxiety about what they leave undone.)

According to the above, it would have been more realistic for a full-time, professionally qualified social worker to recount his or her daily activities over a period of five months. But it is doubtful whether one could make an intelligible, coherent story of scores of highly complex situations picked up, sorted, held or passed on over even a limited period of time. If (like me) the reader is insufficiently adept at mental arithmetic to calculate what is involved, an alternative would be just to think twice before scapegoating a few named social workers in the press after inevitable tragedies occur, and to realize that we are as distressed on these occasions as anybody else, irrespective of whether the tragedy seemed inevitable or could with hindsight perhaps have been averted.

Finally in this introduction, may I set the immediate scene for the diary. My placement in Marlshire was arranged by my tutor as a special treat, partly because it was in a rural area where I would feel at home and be able to draw upon past experience. The group of students met their fieldwork supervisors a few weeks before the placement began—such a meeting being deemed essential by my prospective supervisor, Miss Farrar, who said she could not plan a student's programme without previously 'clapping eyes on her and shaking her by the hand'. It may become apparent that Miss Farrar talks more in terms of plans than of the untidy personalities featured in her forethought. I may as well admit now that, from my viewpoint, I no sooner clapped eyes on *her* than I recognized yet another 'powerful woman' (whose peers, secure in their own successful careers, may be slower to perceive in relation to each other) and literally felt slightly faint at the prospect. However, she proved a lasting tonic in being simply herself until I slowly discovered that any power-fulness was accompanied by depths of unobtrusive kindness and integrity. So she contributed towards counteracting a severe hangover from my previous employment.

The other half of the scene was the University of Barchester but, in the nature of things, it remains in the background of the following pages because these were written initially for private discussion between me and my tutor. So no space is devoted here to the lectures, seminars, discussion groups (revolving round components such as social work methods and values, human growth and 'normal' and deviant human behaviour, social policy and administration, law, social medicine) and individual tutorials, synchronizing with practical experience in the field. That my tutor was an emotionally supportive person, in whom one could safely confide, can probably be read between the lines. It is this one requires above all: a reliable confidant, willing to empathize in the background, if one is to gain confidence in meeting other people's problems in the foreground.

I hope this diary conveys something of the ramifications and fascinations of work in the former child care service, much of which is still relevant today, and may become more so if specializa-tion should increase in future. The complexities of being a student, and of supervising a student, may also emerge. During apprentice-ship in social work, one is rarely observed by seniors at the coal face, which means that the beginner meets a range of new and unexpected situations alone, and the supervisor has to rely on impressions gained at second hand. Typically the student experiences phases of feeling lonely, powerless (thereby tending to invest the supervisor with unrealistic powerfulness at times), doubtful of her ability to offer help to people with very different life-styles, open to disappointment and disillusionment. These are only phases, however, and it would also be true to suggest that students gradually gain confidence through finding themselves effective in small ways which may sometimes need to be pointed out by the supervisor.

I have no more diaries up my sleeve, so no group of people who have so far escaped comment need wonder whether there might be a sparrow among them taking notes from the crumbs they let fall.

Diary

21 March–26 August

21 March

I arrived at 9 a.m. at County Hall in Marlford (the county town) where both the headquarters and the east area of the Marlshire Children's Department are situated; was welcomed by Miss Farrar, my supervisor who is also deputy children's officer, given a desk diary in which I entered every relevant date between now and 26 August at her dictation, was also given a file of useful information, the names of three foster-mothers plus skeleton details of an application for short-stay care; was introduced to Miss Gibbs (east area officer) and four fieldworkers in her team, was taken round the department to meet Mr Tasker (the boss) and what seemed to be about fifteen administrative members of county staff and heard about their functions; was introduced to a selection of official forms beyond my previous imagination, and shown the filing system. . . .

At about 10 a.m. I was told I could 'vegetate for ten minutes' and sank gratefully on to my desk at one end of a large room where all the fieldworkers with Miss Gibbs and Miss Farrar (at the other end) are accommodated together. Had I not already met Miss Farrar once beforehand, I might have thought I'd joined the Civil Service. The rest of the morning is rather a blank. I must have looked at forms and files, knowing I looked pinched (with cold) and unapproachable but unable to do anything about it. The others seemed highly efficient and busy. I was asked to 'gather' in the City Hall garden at 1.50 p.m. for the East Marlshire

Subcommittee meeting, and departed for lunch at 12.45, drove in the general direction of where I imagined the City Hall to be to see where it was, found myself in a large park and wandered lonely as a cloud, in a bitter wind, until I discovered City Hall, walked back by road looking for my parked car (a longish way as the crow didn't fly), nipped into the railway station buffet to buy a sandwich and was dazed enough to try to pay for it with the platform ticket, bolted it and drove to City Hall in time to gather with the others in the garden at 1.50 (cheered by a magnolia tree in full bloom). The worst is over at this point I hope.

The committee meeting was a bit like a film: Lord Brackendale in the chair (constantly seeing himself as a parent to the children in care—which of course he is, statutorily, though it seems unlikely otherwise—and tending to link an eviction with a tied cottage) flanked by Miss Gibbs and Mr Tasker. Other members included Mr Browne on crutches, wanting foster-mothers always to have more money because, one gathered, he himself wouldn't want to do their job at any price, and old Mrs ffrench with moments of practical shrewdness, and watery eyes and hands dripping with diamonds so that one imagines the latter have slowly crystallized through the natural gravity of her teardrops; plus Captain Shaw-Cooper wanting everyone to have less money.

My heart warmed towards the latter (a fellow ignoramus) as he persisted throughout the afternoon in asking a series of unusually silly questions, which made the fieldworkers exchange glances. There is an odd mixture of formality and familiarity through long acquaintance, with extreme tact and skill in the handling of the committee by the officers. This could make for tension: the fear of the officers that issues which mean much to them might be dealt with arbitrarily; that decisions might even be dependent on a rheumatic twinge or the interception of one of the aforementioned glances. But I was struck by the real interest the committee showed, down to the smallest details. There seems to be an art in knowing the optimum amount of information a fieldworker may best report. Everybody has a tacit desire to get through the agenda in a quick, business-like way, but the feelings aroused in different people are often opposing, and rich in variety.

One hears constantly about the amount of emotion generated by the whole subject of children, and this of course applies to the committee even in these dignified surroundings. At one moment

4

they may be discussing a single pair of National Health spectacles and the next moment they come up against something basic like religion or punishment, about which they would probably never fully agree, when the most one can hope for is a grudging compromise from the dissenting member—'All right, but I still don't like it.' Mr Tasker remains calm and wise, and told me afterwards that 'one must be content if the committee makes the right decisions for the wrong reasons'. This is fine, assuming one knows what the 'right decisions' are initially.

22 March

I met Miss Farrar in Marlford at 8.40 a.m. and we went to the north area office for the day. She goes to each of the areas at three-weekly intervals to discuss the work there. I haven't yet gathered how she manages to have such a comprehensive picture of the whole department's work, or what enables the pink memo forms to be so mobile. It would, I think, be simpler to grasp the administrative structure in an area office which is not also the central office.

I took three files with me at Miss Farrar's suggestion (two not directly my business but about children who are to be discussed to-morrow) and tended to get wrapped up in these rather than keep an ear open for the work-conversation which continued steadily all day. I like the way in which Miss Farrar, when discussing the next step for a particular child, thinks it equally important to try to visualize plans and possibilities for that child's long-term well-being. This obviously saves work, worry and energy for all concerned in the long run, although it may seem a fraction unnecessary to a busy fieldworker at the time. One said, 'But I only came back from leave this morning!' All the officers and administrative staff seem to feel quite natural with Miss Farrar (which is more than I do yet, as she is fairly strong meat).

The whole setting seems free from the sort of atmosphere—of uncertainty, edginess and back-biting—which is part of strained working conditions. Extra efficiency (as seems true here) can make work almost impossible and as though the staff had to subordinate their own personalities in order to attain the required standard, but smooth-running machinery can also give freedom to the underlying spirit of the work, enabling it to dovetail securely.

There are enough officers in each area now to cover the work without it getting on top of them, and they have time for frills which must make all the difference to parents, children and foster-parents—for example, taking a little boy, who had proved too much for his foster-family, back to see them for an afternoon so that he shouldn't feel entirely cut off from his past life after moving to a children's home.

The files seem dull at first sight—a collection of forms and official letters plus running report arranged in sequence over a period of years, but it is fascinating to find how a real story slowly develops as you read on—also it helped me to see how these multifarious forms are used. I gather it takes about a year for a new fieldworker to settle in his area and know it thoroughly. Two of the fieldworkers asked me to have lunch with them—one of them was on the same course earlier at Barchester.

23 March

I went in at 8.45 (usual time). Miss Farrar discussed plans for tackling the potential short-stay care case, which I'm to start next week. It's more complicated than I'd expected and the confinement is due on 15 April. I don't quite see myself gaining the co-operation of 'a mother of a well-known problem family' in completing all the necessary forms for receiving her three children into care while she goes into hospital, but suppose it will come clear one step at a time. And you return to the office in between steps.

Then I went with Miss Farrar to the Brayley Children's Home, together with Miss Beckwith (the visitor for this home). I was impressed by it, and by the housemother, Mrs Coombs, who has apparently taken to the life so naturally that local people see her blending with the surroundings. They met this morning to discuss two children living with Mr and Mrs Coombs. The first will leave school in July and, as he wants to work in the south area, his new 'planner' had also come to discuss what he hopes to do. The unmarried mother of the second boy, Kevin, had abandoned him about eleven years ago, and nothing had been heard of her since. He went from a residential nursery to a foster-home; thence to the Reception Centre, then to another foster-home and finally to Brayley, and there was so little likelihood of his ever meeting his mother that he grew up thinking himself an orphan. Miss Beckwith made great efforts to trace his mother, and her success at the end of his file makes exciting reading.

Kevin's mother, mentally handicapped, is now married with two little boys, and her husband knew nothing of the earlier son. Miss Beckwith has been to see them twice (hundreds of miles away); it sounds as though the husband might be valuable to Kevin, and they are willing to proceed as slowly as necessary to synchronize with Kevin's feelings about suddenly having a family. The immediate discussion centred on how and when he might be told. Mrs Coombs, who felt him to need courage and support, is to tell him because she knows him so well, and is available for him to continue to ask questions indefinitely as he digests the news. He is quite a disturbed child who's attended child guidance for several years. Miss Beckwith will go on visiting and keep in touch with all parties. Every aspect was discussed, even to the procuring of a tactful birth certificate should Kevin require proof, and all the possible reactions. It is visualized that he shall meet his family gradually and perhaps be adopted by them in about two years.

Kevin was ten years old before efforts were made to trace his mother. Miss Farrar says this is always the temptation: not to disturb the foster-home that you've planned so carefully and risk losing the child to a less favourable environment. It's too early to know, but I think I shan't feel quite like this. I'm almost sure the actual environment (providing it contains enough good-will) is less important to the child than his need to have a picture of himself (to show to himself and others, particularly other children at school) as somebody who lives with his real mother. The only thing is, will she seem real if she has been unable to do anything for him since giving birth?

Miss Beckwith had lunch with me to explain which of her short-stay foster-homes might be available for the three children in the family I'm to visit next week. Afterwards I read the files of four children in the three long-term foster-homes to be temporarily handed over to me.

I don't see (yet) how anyone scatty could cope with this work, and am beginning to feel grateful to Mrs Strang, who did at least knock a little business-sense into me and the idea of doing things 'immediately if not sooner'.

28 March

I set off first thing to meet this 'well-known problem family' in Crossbridge about twenty miles away. I stopped in a crowded street there to ask a policeman the way—he jumped into the car without being invited and came all the way with me, but I managed to turn him out before we reached the door. The physical conditions in this home are bare but not quite what I'd consider typical of a 'problem family'. But it's certainly a mix-up in relationships. The husband is living with another woman in Marlford. Their eldest child, a son, is permanently with his maternal grandmother in Pilbury in unpleasant-sounding conditions. Mrs Chubb, aged 25, is living with a youth (whom I later discovered to be only 18) who is mentally handicapped and under statutory supervision—he is the father of the coming baby.

Mrs Chubb applied for her three little girls (Linda, aged 5; Susan, aged 4; Tracey, aged $2\frac{1}{2}$) to be received into care during her confinement in hospital. She is said to be unable to read or write —and I'm not sure whether this was an advantage or not as I waded through the RIC (reception into care) form for the first time. It contains numerous questions which seem extraneous when receiving children for only ten days, but one asks them in the knowledge that short-term care not infrequently becomes long-term. When I asked three times whether each of the little girls had been baptized, Mrs Chubb firmly replied 'No' three times, then added 'Only christened.'

29 March

After Miss Gibbs had read my notes and forms, and asked me to telephone some other agencies, she agreed that the three girls should be received into care. I returned to make further plans with Mrs Chubb, but she was out. A public health inspector was also on the doorstep, trying to visit; I learnt that one rarely finds the family at home and that, although they can't read, a letter is the only effective method of communication. So I put a printed note in words of one syllable through the letter-box. Later I visited a fairly new, young foster-mother in Andersham (about fifteen miles from Crossbridge and a similar distance from Marlford) hoping she would agree to take the two younger children. I wasn't prepared for the delight with which she greeted the request. In the evening, I went to see the children's father—out.

30 March

I visited Mrs Chubb again, had a friendly welcome from the children, finished the RIC form, coaxed out information for the three medical forms (translating 'birthmark' as small-pox vaccination), planned clothes and introductory visits to the foster-homes next week, and discussed how Mrs Chubb will explain to her daughters, and help them to prepare. Then I went to see the second foster-mother about two miles away to see if she would take Linda so that she can continue at the same school, and made plans there with Mrs Watson. It is encouraging to find the foster-mothers so helpful, adaptable and pleasant to meet. Apart from transporting a cot, finding clothes, visiting the father, and driving Mrs Chubb and the girls to meet the foster-families next week, it's all tied up—on 12 memo forms (7 visits, 6 telephone calls), 2 RIC forms, 2 letters and 3 medical forms!

4 April

Miss Farrar is away this week and last—it's quite touching to find how her junior colleagues feel responsible for taking a hand in my training, especially while she's away. I've had one or two long lectures about foster-care from the more recently qualified field-workers (who are probably younger than I am). Seven of us work in one large room—I didn't relish telephoning at first under these conditions but am past minding them overhear now—so we come to know a little about each other's cases. There is nothing rigid about the general sharing of foster-homes in any worker's particular patch, so that one is constantly hearing of colleagues' children when visiting, and information is passed on very correctly in a memo to the relevant person.

The fieldworkers are only too willing to tell me about their cases. At first I was surprised, when I made a would-be friendly enquiry about a family, expecting a casual answer, to find that the officer laid down her pen, looked into the middle distance, and proceeded to relate the whole history in an extraordinarily concise, orderly manner with not a word wasted or out of place—just as though

speaking into a dictaphone. I appreciate this, but there is something a fraction impersonal and off-putting about it. Perhaps it
comes partly through practice in dictating records—which will
not come easily to me. But there are one or two aspects of a social
worker's professional persona that I don't much want to acquire—
perhaps it wears off again later.

In fact the newly qualified workers here are markedly more
earnest than those I've met hitherto elsewhere, though it seems
Miss Gibbs has her own slightly sharp humour; also Miss Farrar,
while consistently standing no nonsense, has a rollicking laugh
which reverberates throughout the room, particularly when she
is using her characteristic phrase: 'It went orf at half-cock!'
(though this seems to have a shooting rather than a sexual con-
notation). Before coming here, I gathered from other people that
the Marlshire County Children's Department, while greatly
respected, doesn't let its students off lightly. The chief way in
which this came over to me initially is their tendency to ask rather
sharp, unwinking questions, reminiscent of 'When did you last see
your (foster) father?'

This morning I went to see one of my long-term foster-mothers:
Mrs Almond, who must be in her late 50s, on her own in looking
after a 12-year-old boy, Eamon Murphy. The records aren't very
full, perhaps because it's a child protection case (i.e. a private
foster-home, not under the County Council except for 'supervision'), but it was intriguing to read the brief file over a period of
twelve years and then to meet Mrs Almond in the flesh. Her house
in Drayton is one in a row, with veiled windows, and for many
years she has been taking in unmarried mothers to have their
confinements there. Eamon is the only fish who didn't get
away.

Mrs Almond fixed me with both eyes and told a long story
which she swore several times was the truth if she were to meet
her Maker tomorrow. I found it rather sinister; also she is somewhat pathetic, with more invested in Eamon than she cares to
admit. Eamon's mother, Miss Kathleen Murphy, has visited him
regularly all these years and is supposed to be a difficult person to
deal with, although she was only dealt with once in the records.
Periodically she feels the need to exert her maternal authority
and either moves, or threatens to move, Eamon from Mrs Almond.
The current battlefield is the question of Eamon's following the

RC faith, and this is quite a new pressure on him, which he is said to resent. As I, being a student, have more time than the former fieldworker, I am supposed to settle the RC battle, and meet all the people in the picture and plan some certainties with Eamon and his adults for the rest of his school career and future employment. It is odd the way one is supposed to deal professionally with religion in the child care service, and one wonders what might happen with different colleagues.

In the afternoon I had an hour's interview with Mr Tasker, the county children's officer. He wants to see me again halfway through the placement to discuss legal and administrative aspects. I was taken aback to find the extent to which he was expecting criticism of their organization—it must take months to grasp, I told him, before one is in a position to criticize. He seemed to think I would find it 'authoritarian' (and I suppose it is a bit, once having the word put into my mouth) and that I'd prefer a policy of welcoming every application for care with open arms instead of vetting them carefully as they do. We talked about the amount of responsibility a fieldworker carries in Marlshire.

Apparently responsibility is shared within the department, but can only be so if the worker reports circumstances fully. The same idea continues with the department putting its cards openly on the committee table. There are two opinions about this, Mr Tasker said, but it does act as a safeguard in enlisting committee backing should difficulties arise later. He said 'no fieldworker is asked to go against the feel of her own case' even if a different approach looks advisable on paper to her seniors. The system works so that the upper hierarchy knows what is happening, and Miss Farrar keeps an overall eye on casework throughout the county. He asked me a bit about my previous experience at Downcroft, and we agreed that, though it seems unthinkable (when one is actually working in an approved school) to consider letting the inmates loose into the community, in fact less than a thousand girls in the whole country could be assimilated fairly simply in the outside world without noticeable disruptions—perhaps in ordinary families where selected foster-mothers received unusually high boarding-out rates. He did not go so far as to suggest that he and I should sally forth immediately on a nation-wide operation comparable with Henry VIII sacking the monasteries.

5 April

I was sent to the south Marlshire area to be shown the administrative set-up there by the area officer. It helped, because it's not easy to disentangle the area and central workings in Marlford. The south area possesses a file for students' use containing a copy of every conceivable form, each with explanatory notes typed on it. We made a quick visit to Redlands, the county's reception centre, used mostly for children whose foster-homes have broken down and those committed to care by the courts. It can take up to twenty-two children but has only seventeen at the moment.

Later in the afternoon, back in Marlford, two fieldworkers came in, having gone to visit a foster-home together. They arrived there to find the foster-mother, Mrs Firth, had died suddenly that morning. Her two foster-children originate from a family of six, all of whom Miss Beckwith received into care in her early days here. They are Spanish; soon after immigrating, their father was taken into psychiatric hospital diagnosed as schizophrenic; then their mother was kept in on a similar label when she innocently went to visit him, and it was a few days before neighbours realized the six children were left in their home alone, none able to speak English. At this point Miss Beckwith was called in, managed after a lot of work to board them out in twos in three foster-homes close together, and was just beginning to feel they were happily settled.

Miss Gibbs saw the situation as illustrating that there is no infallible care or security anywhere. 'People say', she said, '"Take them into care away from their parents and they'll be perfectly all right under the local authority's wing until they grow up"—and then the Lord sees fit to remove Mrs Firth. . . .' I thought the staff seemed disturbed by this death beyond the measure of their distress for the foster-mother and her husband, and for the two foster-children in their further loss—because, perhaps, it stressed the uncertainty inherent in one of the most certain parts of the work. At first the unassuming strength of foster-parents is striking to a newcomer, but I suppose one becomes accustomed to it and grows more dependent upon it than one realizes.

In the evening, I went to see Mr Chubb, the father of the potential short-stay children, who is living with another woman in Marlford City, to ask for his consent and to tell him he would be assessed for financial contributions. I thought beforehand that it was likely to be an unpleasant interview and that he'd be on the defensive, but discovered almost immediately that he was thoroughly nervous and apprehensive—too much so to notice that the radio was going full blast and we could hardly hear each other. I could imagine some workers telling him to turn the radio off, but there was such scope for criticism in that house that I ignored it until he suddenly realized it himself towards the end of the interview.

6 April

I'd made a complicated arrangement with Mrs Chubb that I'd call this afternoon so that we could go with the children to meet their foster-mothers, and confirmed this with a printed note asking her to be ready in good time because we had quite a long way to travel. She and the two younger girls were dressed and waiting on her doorstep! Evidently she is very co-operative when she knows what's happening. We drove from Crossbridge to Andersham with Susan (4) and Tracey ($2\frac{1}{2}$) to meet their Mrs Dell, then back to Crossbridge to pick up Linda (5) as she came out of school, and all of us went to Linda's Mrs Watson a couple of miles away.

It mightn't be easy, socially speaking, to do a round of calls with a 'problem family'. The interesting thing to me was seeing how the children rose to (what must have been for them) a most unusual occasion. They had nothing to guide them in their behaviour so were quite natural—quiet at the beginning but soon feeling at home. In both cases it seemed to make a big difference that there were other children already in the homes (foster-parents' own offspring) and they approached each other through the toys. In the second home we found ourselves six children and three grown-ups—the children stared briefly at each other and the next minute were huddled in a group on the floor, crayoning. There may be some advantages in being reared in a problem family, if spontaneous behaviour is not killed by instilling 'nice manners'. Their neighbours refer to these three girls as 'poor little souls' but they seem happy, tough and self-reliant. They made their own overtures to the two foster-mothers, asking direct questions to get their bearings, without going via their mother as more protected children might have done.

During the car journeys in between we talked a lot about the homes, and how they'd played with Trudi in the first, and with Peter and Anne in the second, and of how they'd be going again to stay for about ten days when their mother went into hospital to have a baby. On the final journey, Susan and Tracey made up a little song about Trudi, which they sang until they fell asleep. I found that they tended to identify with the foster-parents' own children—in an attempt, I imagine, to gain some concrete expectations of what life there would be like for a child. They are also intrigued by the subject of fathers, and anxious to know whether the other children had fathers. They regard the boy their mother lives with as 'daddy' although he is only twelve years older than the eldest child.

Mrs Chubb thanked me warmly for having taken them on this jaunt and said how very nice Mrs Dell and Mrs Watson are (very friendly, ordinary countrywomen). This afternoon was the first time (I realized suddenly in the car) I felt to have anything like a relationship with her—previously I felt a bit like an official merely having to assess her 'eligibility' for having her children received into care. She (and the father in Marlford) are wanting to discuss other things, particularly the possibility of a divorce so that each can marry their present partner. The mental welfare officer (when I telephoned him), who supervises the 18-year-old putative father of the coming baby, is alarmed by the prospect of marriage between these two people whose 'combined IQ is only 120!' Not, unfortunately, that there's any such thing as a combined IQ (or fortunately, as academic circles would be intolerable if there were). They do seem though to be very satisfied with their alliance. Mrs Chubb is apparently blissfully unaware of being different from her neighbours. She is rather like some cows I have known— the sort who mean well and bear no malice, but who get much dirtier than the others under the same conditions, and absent-mindedly put their foot in the bucket and have no clue about conforming with the herd, and seem almost more content than the conscientious cows.

At this point, having made other small arrangements about cots, mattresses and rubber sheets, etc., everything is ready for the reception into care. I've stopped bothering about when the confinement is due—the dates are so vague—but others in the department are beginning to be slightly apprehensive lest Mrs Chubb times it for Easter weekend, when I shan't be there.

11 April

I arrived at work quite lit up, having travelled down the valley ten miles from my village lodgings with a rainbow moving alongside, but soon came down to earth during a supervision session (the first really formal one) with Miss Farrar. She aimed at a comprehensive view of my cases with the focus on brass tacks—three-dimensional with regard to time and space and the people involved, including endless attention to small details. At the end, I see there will be no shortage of work. She suggested that I write a social history about Eamon Murphy, bringing it up to date when I've met him, and completing it in August when I have done the foreordained work on the situation (which I privately think may never happen in the manner laid down for me in advance). The file contains factual information relevant to a child protection case but shows little about Eamon and other characters as real people.

Making up for lost time when Miss Farrar was on leave, we had another supervision session in the afternoon when we, using modern teaching methods, literally followed the progress of a Form CHA round the department. Form CHA is used to announce any kind of change in a child's circumstances (of address, planning officer, financial arrangements and so on) and is riddled with little squares, some of which set operations going in other channels.

Miss Gibbs told me in a snatch of conversation that she had bumped into a previous client this lunchtime—a middle-class mother who had earlier placed her baby for adoption. She had now asked Miss Gibbs to call on her over Easter 'in a purely social capacity'. What did I think of this request? Was it superficially a gesture of rewarding Miss Gibbs for her assistance, or a denial of their past relationship with its painful and perhaps guilt-provoking associations? Similarly, Miss Gibbs had recently had a letter from Babs, one of my old farm girls at Downcroft, whom Miss G knew in childhood and who also was responsible for her aftercare. Babs is married now, and wrote to Miss Gibbs, knowing that their statutory relationship is over, saying she would like to keep in touch 'on a social level'. Presumably such requests can sometimes be taken at face value but otherwise may imply a need for further help, particularly as some people only perceive the benefit of support when their compliance as receivers of a service is no longer required of them.

12 April

I'd made plans to visit the other two long-term foster-homes in Drayton but the telephone rang at 9.15. It was a neighbour in Crossbridge to say that Mrs Chubb had gone into hospital during the night, and that she would look after the children until I arrived—great excitement in the office, mainly that I would have the 'pleasure' of putting the previous arrangements into effect. I phoned Mrs Watson and sent a telegram to Mrs Dell, and was in Crossbridge by 10 a.m. plus nine Agreement forms. The children were dressed for the journey and watching for me from the window.

Previously it appeared that neighbours had refused all help because of their disapproval of Mrs Chubb. I'd felt the one weak link in the chain of plans was how the family would notify the department when the time came, and that the scheme would only be foolproof if I either taught Gary, the putative father, how to use a telephone or tied a piece of string to my big toe, but decided they must find a way. And of course when it came to the crunch, one of the neighbours was human enough to want to join in the drama, and/or to heap a piece of burning coal on Mrs Chubb's head and/or felt pity for the 'poor little souls'. So perhaps this shows that one can afford not to make a perfect plan but rather leave room for vaguer elements to coincide, so that other people have scope to help if they wish. Besides this, any plan needs flexibility, and it would go to a social worker's head if her plans continually went like clockwork.

There is a hint of subtle pressure on me in the office suggesting that I should be in control of events, though they must know themselves (and might realize I know too) from everyday experience that this is not possible to the extent they pretend. People seem to vary in the amount they want or need to organize beforehand. There appears to be a happy medium, enabling one to act quickly and effectively in an emergency but not so rigid that one is reluctant to abandon a detailed scheme if it suddenly

16

becomes inappropriate. Sometimes several separate entities seem to move together with surprising harmony; at other times the reverse happens, so one can only wait and see. This Chubb situation did go rather well and I really experienced what it feels like to be a link.

The home seemed more poverty-stricken than before; Gary (whom I haven't yet met) had gone to work hours ago; the neighbour was full of shocked self-righteousness and the children without the clean clothes and change of clothing Mrs Chubb had offered. I took Linda (5) to Mrs Watson first as it's quite near. She shows unusual poise for a 5-year-old and told me immediately that her mother had gone to hospital and seemed glad to go on talking about this and get her facts fitted. She received a warm, unceremonious welcome and I left her happily. Susan and Tracey were more than ready to get in the car. I said to Susan, partly to see the effect of a preliminary visit, 'You know where we're going now?' She replied, 'To play with Trudi.' We spent some of the journey getting things clear while Susan (4) translated to Tracey (2½). Susan obviously felt responsible for Tracey but was mischievous in between. They started off in the back of my old two-door car and finished the fifteen miles together in the front seat, having clambered over, and it was quite a hazardous trip where I could have done with another adult. They settled down with Mrs Dell more or less where they left off the week before and I said I'd visit them tomorrow.

In the afternoon I rang the hospital with a message for Mrs Chubb saying her three daughters were all right, and heard she had given birth to a strong baby girl weighing 8lb. Sister said Mrs Chubb looks ten years younger than at the time of her last confinement—because, she thought, home conditions 'are so much happier'. In the evening I visited Mr Chubb to tell him the children are in care.

13 April

I'd scavenged through the second-hand clothes in the department and selected a quantity for Susan and Tracey. They were physically transformed almost beyond recognition this morning—too much so for my liking, as Mrs Dell had cut their hair and washed it, as well as the clothes they stood up in, overnight. I hope Mrs

Chubb doesn't mind about their new hair-styles; Mrs Dell seemed to have done it in an excess of zeal, perhaps wanting to make her own impression on her foster-children. They were delighted with the clothes (the least motley available) which fitted well. Later I went to see Mrs Chubb in hospital, looking equally scrubbed in a Persil-white nightie. She was glad to hear about the children and to show me her fine new baby. I told her how well she'd timed it—she agreed enthusiastically, and said she was surprised! She wanted to talk about the divorce again. Gary is delighted with the baby (who is to be called Jayne, which may or may not be how Mrs Chubb thinks my name is spelt) and so is Sister, which all offsets the sordid background.

At this point I went off for Easter plus a few days at the university.

25 April

On return I heard that Mrs Chubb had 'behaved like a perfect mother', telephoning three days ago immediately on leaving hospital to ask for her children to be restored to her. She had collected Linda herself the short distance, and I was to return the other two this morning. I thought Mrs Dell seemed a little weary, and intend to visit her next week, but Susan and Tracey were in fine form and high spirits. We had another rather hectic car-journey while Susan chattered almost non-stop about the foster-home and her own home. She summed up the situation of leaving the former by saying, 'Trudi can play with all the toys now.' Again she seemed clear about what was happening, only confused in referring to all her parental figures as mummy and daddy, while I varied between mummy/lady/auntie. The scene when we reached Crossbridge reminded me of the gate being opened between two fields of ewes and lambs which have been separated for the day while the latter are tailed or the former sheared. I went on to see Mrs Watson and thank her, and then celebrated the close of this first short-stay case by having lunch at 11.30 a.m. by a river, dabbling my toes, before returning to complete nine more CHA forms, etc.

In the afternoon I went to the private long-term foster-home again where there is the religious battle. Mrs Almond was just going out, but talked at me through the car window for twenty minutes. Things had come to a head on Good Friday. Eamon's mother, Miss Murphy, had threatened that she would send him to a 'Reform School' if he didn't follow the RC faith. Eamon disappeared to think this over, while Miss Murphy departed to the Stations of the Cross service, and Mrs Almond watched a similar service on TV. Later Mrs Almond told Miss Murphy that at each stage of 'Christ's persecution' she had thought how Miss Murphy was 'crucifying Eamon' in exactly the same way. There is a lot more in it than this, and Mrs Almond's mental health seems to me to be at a low ebb. She reminds me very much of somebody else who had the same cloying sentimentality and who became psychotic (not that it follows) but it's strange how distasteful it is to hear someone slightly off balance talking about religion even if they say the usual things.

26 April

This morning I'd arranged to see Eamon by himself, and am supposed to 'sort it out'. I feel awkward asking him to talk about his religion when he already has two other women (not to mention the priests) pulling at him like birds at a worm. Just before I saw him, Mrs Almond begged me 'not to go too deeply as it will bring on his mental sickness'—he's been having night terrors, and I hope he doesn't have one tonight.

So Eamon and I found ourselves very formally in the front room. He is 12—intelligent, too polite, definite in his ideas and has an odd, detached veneer of hard-boiled sophistication with his strained manner. When I felt I'd catechized him more than enough, I changed the subject, but admired the way in which he answered briefly and returned to finish what he had to say about religion. He added that his mother had always threatened him to get her own way; that this had worked in the past but he now found it 'boring' and she couldn't yet understand the change in him. Afterwards he showed me his sword—given to him yesterday, which demonstration made Mrs Almond very jumpy—and his bicycle, and asked me about my work, wanting to know to what extent I'm a free agent. I didn't say I don't altogether know myself, but tried to convey that I hope people have some personal freedom of choice in matters such as their own religion. Before I went, Mrs Almond, hovering in the narrow hall, apologized for treating me 'as though you don't know better what you're about than I do'—yesterday she called me 'pet' with a good deal of underlying hostility.

At last I visited the other two long-term foster-homes, also scattered in Drayton. One foster-mother is Mrs Yates, a rough old soul whom I liked. She has two foster-children: George Gardiner, aged 13, and Jimmy Best, aged 10. She has had both since they were babies and has met a small procession of social workers over the years—Miss Farrar and later Miss Gibbs used to visit in earlier days. Different workers have strongly opposing views about Mrs Yates, and on several occasions neighbours have written to the department making allegations about her—so some people think she's excellent and others believe she is unfit to have children. I think the reason may be that she enjoys babies more than pre-adolescent boys, because it is the early workers who thought most highly of her.

There is one story of Mrs Yates at her best. Jimmy had been privately fostered as a baby until his mother abandoned him, and was in an extremely poor state (ricketty, physically and mentally retarded through having been kept tied in a pram continuously without exercise) when he was received into care and placed with Mrs Yates. Two workers left him with her and came back an hour or two later to find that she hadn't moved, but was still nursing him because this was what he seemed to need most at the time. Mrs Yates told me today that her doctor thought it unlikely that she would rear Jimmy, 'as he was so terribly neglected', so she is proud to have succeeded. Something I've hardly met before is the foster-mother's formal introduction of her foster-children to a new worker—I imagine this rather stiff few moments dates from the more exclusively inspectorial function of the pre-1948 visitor, and is on a par with looking at school reports, which still seem to be taken quite seriously.

But it seems some foster-mothers enjoy meeting a new worker in some ways—it does give them a chance to tell you the history of their relationship with the child, and to recall ups and downs over the years, and gives you a chance to appreciate their efforts over the entire period, not just for the past two months. Mrs Yates told me this morning that she and her husband would like to adopt Jimmy. This is the first time it has been mentioned, and I'm glad because it will entail more frequent visits with a special purpose. She may change her mind when she realizes that adopting

Jimmy would mean forfeiting the boarding-out allowance, as she is short of money; it would also mean trying to trace his mother who disappeared soon after his birth, and considering the effect upon George. I made few comments today except that I'd return for discussions, not being sure how the department would greet the news, but she talked for a long time about Jimmy.

Possibly a foster- or adoptive mother can never get over the fact that, however much she gives the child during many years, she didn't actually give birth. I felt that what Mrs Yates was trying to explain about the question of adopting Jimmy is that she is confident of having kept him alive where others might have failed, so that in effect he was reborn through her, and therefore she has an unquestionable right to adopt him—a highly convincing argument.

Apparently much of the work with George will consist of helping him in relation to his mother, who hasn't really been encouraged by Mrs Yates and has virtually withdrawn latterly. George discovered he was illegitimate about a year ago, and now prefers to regard Mrs Yates as his mother and has disowned Miss Gardiner. I believe his circumstances were discussed with him at least once but perhaps not enough. Mrs Yates cannot adopt him because Miss Gardiner withholds her consent. It may appear superficially that some foster-children solve their dilemma by transferring affection wholeheartedly to the foster-parents (who must rarely be able to resist this, or the temptation to portray the mother as unfit) yet I'm sure these children can't feel comfortable until they are given opportunities to know, or at least know about, their mother realistically, as a person who contains much that is good.

A child may seem satisfied with a simple attitude of 'Your mother was no good, but you've always got me' (which may be a common stance) but this must be cold comfort in the long run, even though I think prolonged foster-care creates its own genuine bonds. The above is obvious, though one tends to overlook these intangibles when preoccupied with the concrete situation in the foster-home, and it is simpler to deal with the parent-figures on the spot. An added complication is the younger child's black-and-white views, and inability to visualize a situation culminating in his illegitimate birth, though he may always feel his own acceptability is very much bound up with his mother's, even if he doesn't remember her and is never likely to meet her. The thing calculated to hurt even the most hardened approved school girl worst was a critical remark about her parents—I've seen this used as a last resort in trying to gain the upper hand, but it often resulted in the girl throwing a hysterical scene to shut off the words.

The third long-term foster-home is supervised for an authority far away on the south coast. Mr and Mrs Bateson came to Drayton about two years ago; have an adopted son, David aged about 11, and Sally, a foster-child aged 5 whose mother was 'certified as feeble-minded'. Sally is described medically as 'grossly abnormal' —extremely retarded, with a speech defect and unco-ordinated movements, but is said to be a child who inspires affection every-where—particularly in Mrs Bateson, so that David is suffering and showing behaviour difficulties. Mrs Bateson 'would rather have ten Sallys than one David'. Sally started in an ordinary primary school recently and has made strides, but will almost certainly have to attend a residential special school later on. Mrs Bateson is described as quick to take offence, and finds it hard to be separated from Sally even briefly. Sally is fascinating to meet, and goes in for a lot of make-believe play—which would seem to me to offset the label of retardation.

27 April

First had a discussion with Miss Farrar and Miss Gibbs about whether the Chubb family in Crossbridge should be referred to the Co-ordinating Officer, as several agencies are concerned although we have finished, and the family is at a crucial stage. Marlshire County Children's Department doesn't undertake preventive work—I'm glad that Loamshire (where I was appointed last week to start work at the end of August) does. Apparently we shall not attend meetings of the Co-ordinating Committee (if any) but the family is to be referred. Actually the case doesn't close with a snap—small things continue to crop up.

Miss Farrar, in our supervision session, expressed delight over the potential amount of work involved in the three long-term cases, and had anyway thought of several aspects she wanted settled— some administrative. Some concern things one would either ignore or explore thoroughly, according to available time. She thinks it better for me to work intensively on a few cases, although with a full work-load it mightn't be possible to tackle more than a few at a time on these lines. Later she wants to discuss how one would select such cases. (Being Miss Farrar, she is already planning ahead for my future in Loamshire.) She said, for example, that one 'wouldn't touch Eamon's religious problem with a barge-pole unless there were time'. Even if I had a barge-pole, I probably wouldn't want to touch it anyway, but am perhaps getting unnecessarily worked up about it—Miss Farrar sees it from a very practical angle.

I suppose they grow accustomed to it, but I don't care for it in an authoritarian setting. I half agree it's the best thing to do though it seems dangerous when all their feelings are so involved: a stormy mother who is notoriously difficult although (as Miss Farrar says) she's never been approached by us for her own sake and is said to hate us; a 'neurotic' foster-mother who is harping unhealthily; a torn boy who is determined to have freedom of choice and thinks he's already settled it by saying so and who may react badly if the situation drags on; an RC priest whose duty it is to hang on to Eamon; some relatives who side with Miss Murphy; any potential spiritual leaders of Eamon (he intends to do the rounds) to see if they are willing to harbour a lapsed Catholic; the temporary chairman who is RC and likely to recommend some books for Eamon, and me with mixed feelings—it will be quite a miracle if we all emerge none the worse.

Miss Farrar cited other instances to illustrate this difficulty: of mothers who dub the child with some denomination which must later be rigidly carried through in her absence; of adolescent boys who need men teachers but must go to a Catholic school where they play up the nuns, and a mistake made over one little girl who was baptized C of E (I think) but the only suitable foster-home was RC so the committee gave permission for her religion to be changed accordingly—three years later the foster-home broke down and, as there are so few RC homes available, they wanted to change her religion back again, but it's less easy in the reverse direction. If there is something definite in the Regulations, why bother? But if one's attempting casework inside the framework, what then?

Next I listened (mainly) to the six-monthly review on Sally, and then wrote up yesterday's interviews. I have a new short-stay application to investigate. It sounds simpler than the last—only one child, the youngest of five, who was nearly received into care once before so there is past information, and it sounds a less complex family, except that the child is car-sick. The administrative side seemed daunting last time, but I shall feel quite different about it this time.

2 May

I'll give the whole story of this potential short-stay case as it happened during one and a half days, because it was so enjoyable. I went to the village of Long Winkley (about ten miles away) this morning to meet the mother, Mrs Ethel Rock. She expects to go into hospital for a hysterectomy quite soon and will be away four to five weeks. She is a gaunt-looking countrywoman with no top dentures and five children—four schoolboys and the youngest, Jenny, is 4 years old. Mrs Rock started by hoping the three youngest children might be received into care. (At first one is keeping a mental ear open to department policy, so that you're almost holding an inward conversation with the hierarchy while talking outwardly with the parent miles away, but it suddenly seems much simpler if you feel free enough to create a plan with the mother inside your framework like any normal human being.)

After some discussion about past arrangements, we decided that Mr Rock could manage to look after the four boys if he went to work at 9 a.m. instead of 7 a.m. with his foreman's permission. He is a roadman for Marlshire County Council and is also able to do housework with slow willingness, in rather the same spirit, I imagine, as he attends to stretches of hedges and banks. A neighbour has offered to keep an eye on the family at home, so it seemed at this stage that Jenny was our main consideration. Mrs Rock and I began to fill in the RIC form together. (When I asked, 'And are you Church of England too, Mrs Rock?', she replied, 'Yes, please.') One section requires names and addresses of relatives, plus reasons why they cannot offer care. Mrs Rock gave me details of two sisters and two sisters-in-law, all of whom sounded to have genuine reasons. It looked clear to me that Jenny would need our care, but I told Mrs Rock I'd come back after discussing it in the office, and asked whether she and Jenny could visit a prospective foster-home with me tomorrow if necessary.

I returned to Marlford; wrote up the interview, thinking to myself what I'd do next and that I'd have it all sewn up in no time, so I'd counted unhatched chicks by the time (lunch-time) I handed the report to Miss Gibbs for approval. Miss Gibbs said 'Hmm. . .'; that we were tending to take relatives' excuses too easily without full investigation, so would I see the relatives next. This put out my calculations, and I rushed back to tell Mrs Rock, having sandwiches in a wood on the way there. She thanked me without much heart—I gather there is extended family-feeling but that it's complicated by Mrs Ethel Rock being less worthy than some members, by prolonged reactions to a contested Will, by the distances involved in travelling within a radius of about twenty-five miles, and by the amount of illness.

Then I did the rounds, in lovely country and a small thunder-storm:

(a) Mrs Clara Rock in a farm cottage, over 60, with a lot on her plate and a husband recovering from an accident to his face, working part-time. She badly wanted to help, because Mrs Ethel had 'once helped me when I was in great trouble', but saw her share as hospital-visiting (long distance) and a few meals for the boys. We called her husband in from the farm and they each wanted the other to decide. Finally we sat in silence for a few minutes while Mrs Clara struggled with her conscience—it came over her face in conflicting waves as she glanced alternately at her husband and me, like a spectator of a slow game of tennis. So I said I didn't see how they could manage to have Jenny, partly through wanting to get them off the hook and partly because it does seem that people sometimes can only say yes after one has allowed them to say no first. We left it that the answer was prob-ably no, but that they'd ring up before Wednesday if they changed their mind.

(b) Mrs Gladys Rock—in Long Winkley, several miles from Mrs Ethel as it's a straggly village but the nearest relative; suffering from neuralgia and the installation of a bathroom, and jealousy (according to Mrs Ethel). On finding Mrs Gladys, I discovered that I'd stopped to ask her the way that morning and had thought then how happy she looked—a large, jolly woman with a loud voice and ability to tell a good story; her husband 'Perce' is a baker's roundsman. They adopted Stephen six years ago as a baby —no children of their own. Mrs Gladys couldn't be called a client though she badly wanted to be, and had perhaps missed the social workers she met over the adoption. She told me without

25

encouragement about her neuralgia, bathroom, the family, her childhood, Perce and her marriage, and the story of Stephen's adoption—very interesting. 'That first three months' waiting is hell, isn't it?', she commented. She wanted to discuss her present difficulties with Stephen; it sounds as if she is over-anxious to do the right thing, forcing information on Stephen in prematurely large doses. She thinks constantly of his mother—'On his birthdays and Christmas Day, as soon as I wake up I wonder if his mother's thinking of him—"Stephen's 5 now, or 6"—and I'm always wanting to go and tell her about him and see what she's like. . . .' This long conversation had a direct bearing on Jenny because Mrs Gladys thought a temporary sister would benefit Stephen. It seemed (from other evidence) that her own inability to have children compared with Mrs Ethel's five reproductions is a source of great pain. We left it that she'd discuss the possibility of Jenny overnight with Perce and ring me at 9.00 the following morning.
(c) Mrs Pickett (sister) in Crale St Theresa—oldish, with a TB spine and a delicate husband. Here it was quite obvious that she would have had Jenny had it not been impossible. She told me about her illness and what it meant, and how it might affect Jenny—i.e. that she is unsafe with a child because of sudden blackouts and a tendency to be irritable through constant pain. She was glad to hear news of the rest of the family.
(d) Mrs Dacey (sister) in Darvey Crale. She lives in a row of really beautiful council houses with a Georgian flavour. She is over 60, in poor health, with a husband who's been off work for four years with 'nerve trouble' and arthritis. She had never seen Jenny, was very interested but obviously couldn't help directly. She told me about their mother's maxims for housekeeping— there was rather the same wholesome smell in the three sisters' houses, miles apart.

By this time I was tired, though enjoying being able to give news around the circle of family members who so rarely meet but remain concerned, and it was surprising to realize I'd never met any of them until this very morning.

3 May

At 9 a.m. Mrs Gladys rang up and said they'd be glad to have Jenny, on one important condition: that her parents paid for her keep—as a 'matter of principle really' (and perhaps as a forfeit for having five children). I discussed this with Miss Gibbs. I felt that Mrs Ethel might easily be unwilling to let Jenny go to Mrs Gladys, who gave me a vague impression that she'd tend to take in Jenny as an amoeba ingests its food. ('It's a little girl I've always really wanted.') Miss Gibbs said bluntly, 'In that case you say good-bye to Mrs Rock and tell her it's been nice knowing her—you've got to learn to be "nasty" in this work.' I knew what she meant, and replied with some dignity that I'm quite capable of being nasty. 'I'm delighted to hear it', and she called out this information to Miss Farrar, who made no obvious reply. (In fact I attained a terrible height of firmness in approved school work, but haven't yet quite been able to redesign this for social work.)

The next stage looked delicate—it seemed to involve travelling between Mrs Ethel and Mrs Gladys until they arrived at a mutually satisfactory payment-agreement. If this was impossible, I'd have to decide on the spot to receive Jenny into care so that Mrs Gladys would get a boarding-out allowance, but Miss Gibbs hoped this would prove unnecessary. I drove out to Long Winkley, and told Mrs Ethel the position. She'd just had a letter asking her to go into hospital tomorrow. Her husband didn't know yet, and anyway she must decide with him whether they wished Jenny (who was usually out playing when I went) to go to Mrs Gladys. We discussed it a little, and agreed she couldn't manage to pay more than £1 a week for five weeks for Jenny's keep.

I wanted to see her husband too, so we left car-sick Jenny with the neighbour and set off together to look for Mr Rock. We drove up hill and down dale through tortuous little lanes (getting stuck in a ditch after drawing in for a tractor, and were pushed out by the tractor-driver) and eventually sighted a red flag which meant her husband was in the vicinity and a second red flag which declared we were hot on the trail. We met Mr Rock sweeping steadily on a steep incline—a real roadman except for his trilby hat and horn-rimmed glasses, and we put our heads together on this lonely road. He kept hold of his broom in case his foreman appeared. We ran through the plans and decided he can cope with the four boys and Jenny could go to Mrs Gladys for £1 a week. Mr and Mrs Rock seemed to understand each other with few words. I explained we hoped Jenny wouldn't need to come into

27

care, but asked him to sign an RIC form just in case, to save another journey. He signed with great pains on the car bonnet.

Then, as it was all suddenly rather urgent, Mrs Ethel and I drove to see Mrs Gladys. Mrs Ethel told me about homes and inhabitants as we threaded our way through Long Winkley. She seemed uneasy on entering Mrs Gladys's smarter house, and the latter had a slight air of triumph. She agreed straightaway to accept £1, telling us how pleased Stephen is and how he'd ear-marked a teddy-bear to lend Jenny. Mrs Ethel took time to warm up, so I gave them the extended family news from yesterday. By then the two women were exchanging their own news, and seemed to have met rarely in the past. Soon they were rattling away making plans for Jenny. I didn't join in as it was no longer my business, though it was interesting to hear what a comprehensive discussion they had in broad Marlshire dialect. I wondered how it might have differed had it been a three-cornered conversation on a preliminary visit to a registered foster-home, and whether the mother would have felt as free under those conditions to enlarge upon the sort of care most suitable for Jenny.

Mrs Gladys's contributions had a textbookish air—she was almost advocating Winnicott's transitional love objects unwittingly while Mrs Ethel was right down to earth in describing Jenny's simple needs. They arranged that 'Perce' would go with Mrs Gladys this evening to fetch Jenny in the bread van and that, as Perce delivers bread there three times a week, there would be steady communication between Jenny and her father and brothers at home. Mrs Gladys insisted that any child she took into her home would have to be regarded as hers while it was there (she told me yesterday she could never foster); Mrs Ethel ignored this with the same gaunt dignity she shows about going into hospital. Eventually Mrs Gladys said that poor Miss Sparrow couldn't get a word in edgeways! I said there was no need, because my part was over, and I'm glad they've been able to arrange it between them. Mrs Gladys asked me to continue visiting but I explained why not. We heard some amusing stories of Stephen, and left pleasantly.

As I drove Mrs Ethel home, we passed Mr Clara Rock, returning from the doctor's (six miles away) by tractor. We stopped to tell him the final arrangements; he said his wife would be relieved but would do her bit in other ways. I sent a message to his wife plus a selection of extended family news, in which he was interested though he has a disconcertingly blank face with its injury. I left Mrs Ethel at her home—she seemed philosophical and even happy about the plans, and asked me whether I'd visit her in hospital. I explained I'm sorry I probably cannot as Jenny isn't in care, but said I'd think about her.

As I drove through the long village for the last time, I was beginning to know a few people in passing and almost to recognize some of the sheep by sight. At the far end of the village I passed Mr Clara Rock on his tractor listening hard to Mrs Gladys —they waved until I rounded the corner.

I got back to Marlford at lunch-time and was just going to ring the almoner who referred Mrs Rock, when she rang the department, full of another potential short-stay case—a little boy whose mother goes into hospital today. I took down the details on a memo form but it wasn't allocated to me. I finished recording the Rock situation, and began trying to make an appointment with the NSPCC Inspector who is my next step with Eamon Murphy, simply to discuss the NSPCC's past knowledge. At 5 p.m. I went, with some apprehension, to Miss Murphy's address in Marlford city. She works as a ward-maid and has not hitherto been visited in her flat. I could get no answer from the flats, so waited for half an hour in the car outside with one eye on the door and one eye on a detective story, feeling a bit like a detective myself.

When a man went into the house, I found from him that Miss Murphy no longer lives there but in the residential quarters of the hospital. She would obviously hate to be sought out there as, however careful one was, she might feel the secret of her illegitimate sons was coming dangerously close to her bread and butter. So I'm writing to ask her to come to the office at her convenience. I'm rather sorry it has to be the office—she came there once or twice about seven years ago—it can't have pleasant associations for her.

At that time, Miss Murphy had just had her second son, Shaun, and was behaving in a way which sounds unlikely on paper. In his first few months she moved him round a succession of private foster-homes (at least six) in a manner which made the various social workers' hair stand on end. She was interviewed in the office, and wouldn't accept any suggestions, saying Shaun was her child and no one should take him from her although she wasn't able to look after him herself. Our training is supposed to give us some idea of the motivating forces underlying human reactions and interactions, so we should be able to predict a little—but I defy anybody to predict a panic-stricken mother's movements. All one knows is that anything may happen—often a series of contradictory actions reflecting her inner pulls. On the other hand Miss Murphy is remarkably regular in her work and has held the same job for many years. (Shaun lives with his maternal aunt and her husband, without the department appearing to have a responsibility now.)

4 May

I visited Mrs Dell in Andersham who looked after Susan and Tracey, because she seemed untypically moody on the day I took them home. If it was something upsetting about the foster-children, I wasn't sure whether they'd been too much for her or not enough. She is about 24, but seems younger in some ways, and has only recently become a foster-parent. It's perhaps that she's still unsure of herself, and thinks we demand an impossibly high standard, so that although she appeared to manage extremely well she is still needing to make small confessions about occasions when she could only use her own initiative. I'd thanked her verbally and by letter but she didn't seem satisfied until we discussed the experience thoroughly this morning—the first time we weren't surrounded by children. The main part of the interview out-textbooked any theoretical case which is something quite foreign to my previous conversations. It seemed genuine enough at the time but sounded corny when I tried to record it in the office, so I won't repeat it now.

Later I had a long discussion with the NSPCC inspector, Mr Worth, who knows Eamon, Miss Murphy and Mrs Almond better than I do yet. It helped to talk with someone more objective than I am, as he isn't directly involved nowadays. I recorded most of what he said but prefer to learn more at first hand myself gradually. It was encouraging to discover that Mrs Almond makes him feel uncomfortable too. We think Eamon very much wants to be with her (or thinks he does) but . . . I just stopped myself from saying, 'I couldn't live with Mrs Almond, could you ?'—the very idea would have put him off his lunch.

9 May

Started with supervision. Miss Murphy wrote to me this morning, saying she'd come to the office at 11.30 a.m. There is a lot about her in the file (mostly that she's a 'congenital little liar' whatever that may mean) but it's all hearsay except for one angry interview which was, Mr Tasker says, before the 'shouting technique' went out of vogue (when one bludgeoned as much as possible in the hope that a fraction of what one said would stick).

Miss Murphy came early to the interviewing room and stayed for just over an hour, during which we went hammer and tongs except for two long silences. I felt she could have treated me to more fireworks than she actually did but it was too Irish to reconstruct a coherent record afterwards. We got on better than I'd expected, and you couldn't have two more different women than mother and foster-mother but if you were assessing their 'workability' (to use a horrid word of Perlman's which sounds like dough) I should think in both cases it would be nearly nil. Underlying Miss Murphy's extravagances was a sort of quiet and desperate wish to be recognized as Eamon's mother. She feels she has lost him to Mrs Almond (whose strategy has more guile) and that all she has left is her maternal authority, but her hysterical use of it is fatal. Both women are frightened of each other, jealous and hostile—so it's ugly. Each would use me to hit the other.

In her calmer moments Miss Murphy showed me photographs of the boys as babies and their fathers, and a long letter from Mrs Almond—written just as she speaks. (I remember one bit: 'It is not fair on my Health, and I feel, deep in my Heart, that it is time I put my foot down, on everyone.') I don't know that we got anywhere, but she said she wants to come again. The only hope I see is that, if I recognize her as Eamon's mother, she may have less need to thrust it down his unreceptive throat, which would (particularly from Eamon's side) perhaps enhance their long-term relationship.

In the afternoon we went to Brayley Children's Home for the East Marlshire Area Committee, followed by the Case Subcommittee meeting (2–5 p.m.). I reported the bit about the Chubb children's short-term care. The usual chairman, Mrs Armstrong, is a brisk little body who seems to know, or remember, all the children mentioned; her immediate reaction to any child's setback is a heartfelt 'Oh, dear', which sometimes seems suitable and sometimes incongruous. I do like watching the mixture of committee and officers.

10 May

A day in Drayton, by the river in between visits. In the morning I visited Mrs Yates about a few practical things, and to clear the ground for further discussion about the possibility of their adopting Jimmy. First, she knows the boarding-out allowance would cease and doesn't mind. Second, she'd thought (or hoped) that Jimmy's mother was dead, but understands we shall have to try to trace her (last heard of in a mental hospital hundreds of miles away eight years ago). Third, she and Mr Yates would like to adopt George too if his mother will consider it, and in any case are worried about his relationship with his mother—at the moment it's lapsed. They want not too little, not too much . . . so. . . .

In the afternoon I visited Mrs Almond. I'm at a loss here—she's clever without being intelligent, never stops talking in a most domineering way hidden under sugary sweetness. There's nothing I can get hold of because she is determined to demonstrate that she's doing her utmost 'to keep mother and son together' and would, I think, collapse rather than see differently; also, it's all so sentimental and slightly off-key that one gets no cue for reply. I think she's frightened of my just visiting, which makes her condescending and subtly hurtful in between her sickly endearments. No doubt the textbook answer would be to say, 'I wonder why you feel so . . ., etc.', but I feel I'd need psychiatrists posted all round the house first, ready to burst in at the psychological moment (* see p. 36!).

I learnt that 'all children have feelings'; that Miss Murphy 'must learn to be less un-Christian—I have many faults, but *that* is not one of them.' She asked me, 'I wonder if you have any *conception* of a mother's feelings for her son?' and continued in the same breath, 'Don't answer me! I shouldn't have asked you that question. I *am* so sorry. I *do* apologize. It was *very* wrong of me, because you aren't a mother and can *not* understand. I *am* a mother and I *know* . . . but etc.' I'm afraid my reaction was to look out of the window. She's probably been using that line on a

succession of fieldworkers ever since she saw the first one flinch.
It's a long time since I've met anyone so unlikeable and yet at the
same time she's pathetic which makes it worse. She gives me the
same feeling I used to have when killing poultry or castrating
piglets, and I somehow minded killing an ill one more than a
healthy one. Nothing looks sicker than a sick hen, and the act of
killing something brings you into a horribly close relationship
with it just when you don't want to be.

(I find people tend to be shocked, on the rare occasions I
mention it, that I've done such things frequently in my former
career. However, in practice I found it preferable to know I had
an efficient, instantaneous method of killing poultry of any size
rather than suffer the horror—which happened three times in
my experience—of initially gratefully accepting the offer of
apparently tough men who thought it unsuitable 'for a girl to do
it', and then twenty minutes later to feel the half-plucked bird on
one's knee regaining consciousness, not dead at all—that brought
me out in gooseflesh myself. Similarly, if one is rearing baconers,
one is inevitably involved in castrating piglets—i.e. in holding
them even if the vet does it expensively, and I found that piglets
recovered from the operation more quickly when I did it myself,
partly because they were only separated from the sow for a
few minutes instead of perhaps half-a-day while awaiting the
vet.)

Anyway (as neither Mrs Almond nor Eamon risk anything
quite so drastic) I arranged to go back later the same afternoon
to see Eamon after school. I was allowed to see him alone, but
kept it short for obvious reasons. He looks well, and Mrs Almond
says he's 'a different boy', much happier—I hope so. In between
all this, we do move slightly on a business-like religious plane.
Next week the RC priest may come into the picture. Other
uncomfortable feelings I have about this situation are:

(a) How far do the people believe I've got statutory powers I (and
the department) haven't got?

(b) With a really firm push from me might Eamon return to
RCism? Or would it be the last straw? He seems absolutely
decided and needs support either way. Which would be the most
strain and how much more can he take?

(c) How to be honest with them all.

(d) Having started, I have to go on, but is my reluctance due to muddled thinking or 'over-involvement', or is it really more complex in fact than it looked on paper originally?

(e) If it was left to develop naturally how would it be different? If at all?

(f) How is the fieldworker who said, 'I hope you'll tie it up and hand it back to me on a plate at the end of August' going to feel when she gets it back in September, its last state possibly worse than its first?

I'm not half as worried as this sounds, for various reasons.

11 May

First got up to date with paperwork in the office. From 11.30 for the rest of the day we had a county departmental staff meeting, partly to discuss problems of Part III accommodation for homeless families. At lunchtime I saw a little drama outside the county prison gates which may have been a wife meeting her husband on release—elaborately casual on the surface, quite intense underneath—on the other hand it might simply have been the Governor going for lunch.

16 May

I had a word with Miss Farrar about a few things, and told her I am finding the Eamon Murphy case difficult. Previously I was puzzled because no one in Marlshire seemed to think Mrs Almond half as odd as I do, so I wrote restrainedly about her lest it was 'just me'. However, Miss Farrar said Mrs A is 'coming out in her true colours at last as a devil', and that this hadn't happened in the past because she'd been met more casually and, whatever happens next, it's as well to know. . . . I was just orientating myself towards arranging a meeting with the RC priest when Mrs Almond telephoned me—not surprisingly, because it seemed inevitable that when mother and foster-mother combined at the weekend, each having let off only a fraction of their ill-feeling separately to me during last week, there would be an explosion.

Mrs Almond is highly upset. It seems Miss Murphy has a week's holiday and took Eamon to see some relatives deemed 'taboo' by Mrs A. This led to a scene and the usual threats from both women which are so disturbing to Eamon. What I'd feared was Miss M trying to frighten Mrs A by boasting that I was definitely on her side (although Mrs A would 'know' I'm on her own side because she's under the illusion that she's always right). If Miss M had been cleverer, I think she'd have taken this line because it might have made more trouble; instead she has told Mrs A that she won't have 'welfare' interfering, and that she and I didn't agree. We didn't agree of course, though from my viewpoint we got on surprisingly well on the level of agreeing to disagree. But Mrs A replied that 'the little lady (me) is doing her best for all of us, and she could be your (Miss M's) best friend.'

Mrs Almond talked over the telephone for a long time—half-hostile because I'm vaguely behind this latest outbreak and half-begging for support: 'Miss Sparrow, my dear, I'm at the end of my tether—it is Miss, not Mrs, isn't it?' The upshot is that Mr Tasker, impressively, has offered to accompany me to Drayton to visit Mrs Almond tomorrow. I'm relieved about this—both to have a second first-hand opinion (I almost hope he finds it difficult to get a word in edgeways) and because it is now openly acknowledged that Mrs Almond is not altogether desirable as a foster-mother. I wonder what leads her to specialize in private confinements for unmarried mothers; she does seem to enjoy some power over these women.

11 a.m. Attended a meeting of the Children's Committee—fascinating—the things discussed, and the various people and their attitudes to a variety of situations. As Mr Tasker says, committees tend to dwell on the items you'd expect them to pass over quickly and vice versa.

P.m. continued in the office, writing a social history for Jimmy, and picking out anything in the file which might help in tracing his mother. Further discussion with Mr Tasker and Miss Farrar about Eamon. I can't see any simple solution to Eamon's dilemma. There is vague talk of his being received into care while another, better, foster-home is found. But Mrs Almond is the person he wants to stay with—the sad thing is that he has had no better experience elsewhere to stretch his wishes. If he were moved by us, he would be Section 1 of the 1948 Children Act, with his mother unwilling to co-operate, and Mrs Almond angling to get him back (as she has at least twice before) and having a strange influence over Miss Murphy. If he stays where he is, things are unlikely to change except perhaps to deteriorate. When it comes to the point we have no power to ensure that Mrs Almond can keep Eamon even if we wanted her to, yet Mrs Almond is, in her own way, begging for help, which is why she gives me the feeling of a sick hen.

17 May

Continued Jimmy's social history, and went to another department to see if the section responsible for collecting parents' financial contributions had any information about Jimmy's mother—it hasn't.

P.m. Mr Tasker (a slightly hair-raising driver) and I went to Drayton to see Mrs Almond. She talked non-stop for nearly half an hour before he attempted to speak to her, and she held most of the floor for the next sequence of nearly an hour. But I felt it was a most useful interview. When he did speak, Mr Tasker was very gentle with her, and helped her to face the fact that there is no simple solution so things are bound to continue uncomfortably. Over the weekend she seemed to have transferred some of her former fears to Miss Murphy's 'taboo' relatives but by the end of this interview she was a fraction less rigid in her attitude to them, and intrigued by the idea that Miss Murphy might be jealous of her. Miss M meanwhile, having had her maternal fling over last weekend, is behaving 'as though nothing had happened'. Mr Tasker thinks Mrs Almond needs gradually to recognize her own mixed feelings towards Miss M, though she is well aware as far as I can see, but it might be a step forward if she were less self-righteous in condemning Miss Murphy's occasional outrages.

*(see p. 32)   Funnily enough, I did hear Mr Tasker saying at one point, 'I wonder why you feel so . . .', but there was no need for psychiatrists to rush in—she simply didn't hear. I thought the way Mrs Almond said goodbye to me was rather typical. She gripped my hand with both her hands, scratching me slightly in the process, and whispered, 'God bless you' fervently. She goes in for an unusual amount of hand-holding, and unfortunately I've a slight physical antipathy towards her. On the return journey Mr Tasker thought the most we can hope for is just to keep things ticking over. Miss Murphy has the last word as things stand, and tends to move her sons rapidly from pillar to post once she panics. The only other possibility which might work if Mrs

36

Almond's health deteriorates further is for Eamon to attend a grammar boarding school, returning to Mrs Almond for holidays.

Anyway, I don't mind being sandwiched in this situation any more, now that it's recognized to be complex and delicate—previously I had an impression (perhaps unfounded) that I was expected to tidy it up quickly, which seemed impossible.

18 May

A.m. went to Brayley Children's Home with Miss Farrar, Miss Beckwith and Miss Young (psychiatric social worker at the child guidance clinic) for another discussion about Kevin. He has met his mother and her new family now, and things are moving more swiftly than was originally visualized. They discussed whether it's preferable to hang on to the slow-introduction idea with Kevin perhaps feeling that the department (previously his only reliable stand-by) is keeping him away from his 'parents', or whether to let Kevin live with his far-away family sooner, hoping that it won't break down, with Miss Beckwith and Mrs Coombs remaining in touch.

P.m. supervision session. My course-tutor from the University of Barchester visited, to discuss my progress separately with Miss Farrar and me. Apparently the department finds (or found?) me very reserved, and 'so apprehensive initially' that this made 'all the fieldstaff feel apprehensive too'. I'm sorry (it's partly a hangover from Downcroft) though I don't see why the primmer fieldworkers here couldn't have unbent a little themselves in trying to make me feel more at home. My tutor has thrown considerable light on the Almond-Murphy situation too, so I'm now almost looking forward to meeting Mrs Almond next time.

23 May

The RC priest is away on holiday; I arranged to visit Eamon's headmaster later this week.

I'm getting on with tracing Jimmy's mother, and have written to the public health department in the far-northern city asking if they have any trace as Miss Best was supposed to be in a mental hospital there eight years ago.

This morning I decided to go and see Mrs Phear who features at the beginning of Jimmy's file nearly ten years ago—it was at her ramshackle cottage that Miss Best left him when she deserted, and where he was neglected. In the past, Mrs Phear is the only person who has had news or rumours of either parent. Eventually I found her cottage in a wheatfield about twelve miles away, but the occupants told me she'd left there two or three years ago, and has moved again since, about six weeks ago, and they thought she lived somewhere on Low Flatts. I discovered this to be an ill-defined region of the river in Marlford and wandered for two hours looking for her.

I parked my car where the proper road ends, and asked a very grimy old man for directions. Nobody seemed to know. There were groups of cottages (many condemned) all along the river bank, so I asked at both ends of each group whether a neighbour had moved in recently; also asked at the pub and the lock-keeper's cottage, and along the side-streets at right-angles. At the furthest point, I learned that there was a Miss Darcy nearby 'who knows a lot'. Her house is along an overgrown snicket, with an odd ivy-covered tunnel from front entrance to back. Miss Darcy and the furniture must have been very smart once but now give the impression of having decayed undusted for decades.

I found that Mrs Phear and her daughter live next door—in the most dilapidated cottage I've ever seen. She was more surprised to see me than I was to see her, and looked extremely ill and emaciated in ragged clothes. She had no news, except that her daughter, who works in a factory nearby, thought she'd recognized Jimmy's putative father there a few weeks ago. Mrs Phear and her hysterical dog put me on the trail for the factory; I asked at each of four sections whether anyone of his name was working there. There was no employee of that name and never had been. As I walked back a different way to my car, I met the same grimy old man from the beginning, who wanted to know if I'd been successful in whatever I was looking for. I've always tended to have pleasant little adventures like the above, and am pleased to find they don't decrease with age, and that they're not lacking in the child care service.

Later in the afternoon I went on my first attempt to select potential foster-parents: Mr and Mrs Tolley, who had simply phoned, giving their name and address, expressing interest in fostering. Beforehand I wanted to sit and think in the car for a few minutes about the coming interview because I felt very vague but, as the Tolleys live about seven miles from anywhere at the bottom of a murderous farm-track, the immediate objective rapidly dwindled to a mere desire to arrive at all. It is a delightful thatched farm-house. The first thing to happen was that two well-grown bottle-fed lambs seized the opportunity to nip into the fenced front-garden when Mrs Tolley came out to meet me. At that moment I felt far more competent to catch sheep than to vet prospective foster-parents, so we turned them out of the garden in double-quick time, and Mrs Tolley wondered if I was from the Children's Department or the Ministry of Agriculture, and it became a really enjoyable interview.

I've thought for some time that there are parallels between fostering children and a shepherd's methods with deprived lambs. A psychiatrist in my previous child guidance placement was interested in the possible overlap between a sheep's and a human mother's rejection of her offspring, and I think Bowlby might find it more fruitful to move on from ducks and geese. Sometimes an ewe will have no dealings with her lamb, and the shepherd undertakes rather authoritarian preventive work by penning the ewe several times a day, forcing her to stand still and suckle the lamb. It's a battle of wills—sometimes the ewe gives in with a bad grace, but often she becomes even more stubborn, so the shepherd has to choose one of his methods for orphan lambs.

If a ewe has enough milk to take a foster-lamb in addition to her own, she is selected. If she's just lambed, the shepherd rubs the foster-lamb all over with the after-birth, and usually the ewe is successfully fooled into believing she produced him herself. The smell seems to matter most. If an 'own' lamb dies at a few days old, he is skinned, the foster-lamb is dressed in the dirty, outsize woollen skin, tied under the middle, and the ewe doesn't seem to notice the difference. After a few days, when the foster-lamb is impregnated with the smell of the dead lamb's skin, the coat is removed and they settle down. What most farmers do their utmost to avoid is bottle-fed lambs: they may be sweet to start with but seem unable to grow up normally, so that you finish with a silly sheep who clings to your apron-strings and can't mix with its own kind.

39

Once at Downcroft I set a hen's broken leg and let her stay close to us in the farm-yard while it healed. After several weeks she irritated me by continually getting under my feet and distracting the girls from their work, so I told them she was getting above herself; that it was high time she rejoined her sisters, and remembered she was a hen, not one of us. In spite of protests all round I firmly put her back in the hen-run where she belonged, but I had to give in after two days when she stood glued in the corner nearest the farm-yard hopping wildly to attract our attention when anybody approached—and she came back to get under my feet and distract the girls, living happily ever after until she died a natural death years later and was buried with a ceremonious funeral. If it's true that a horse reaches its highest peak of development when it's at its most horse-like, the same is true of humans—and I don't think an animal develops properly cut off from natural ties, or that a human being striving for saintly qualities (e.g. Mrs Almond, except that she 'goes orf at half-cock') necessarily reaches a superior plane.

So it interested me to talk about these bottle-fed sheep with Mrs Tolley, and to wonder inwardly why she hadn't persevered in fostering them in the usual way. It isn't necessarily significant, but if you didn't know about farming you wouldn't know what shepherds do, and if you weren't training for social work you might know less about parent-child relationships, and if you hadn't done a bit of 'casework' you perhaps wouldn't fit the two together. The Tolleys also have an 18-year-old dog who looked in a poor state possibly with kidney trouble, whom they can't steel themselves to have 'put to sleep'. This again is unusual for farming people, who tend to be matter-of-fact to the point of callousness about life and death; it might possibly be indicative of sentimentality or of real concern for the dog.

Mr Tolley (white hair, blue eyes, pink cheeks) came in and we talked for an hour in the farm-kitchen. Mrs Tolley started the interview proper by saying: 'I'll be quite frank with you—I want a foster-child for companionship.' He started by saying he'd want it definitely understood that any child they had would be theirs for keeps, but he climbed down rapidly when his wife and I had had our say. I liked him very much—the sort of man, I think, that children take to immediately. They both told me their ideas about caring for children, and about their own families and upbringing—in fact they more or less volunteered most of the information I might have decided to seek had there been time to collect my wits in the car beforehand. It did strike me how much richer a life they lead than most clients. But the number of children in the picture seemed almost too much at times.

They have a 'foster-child' aged 28 (inherited from Mrs T's mother) now in Africa, two sons aged 20 and 18, one in the Army nearby and one at home, also her niece Cathy, aged 17. Cathy's mother was apparently 'not a helpful influence' so the Tolleys took her on a year ago. They described her appearance and wild behaviour on arrival, and the change in her since and how this had been achieved. Then there were three evacuees of his mother's during the war, and occasional babies to stay since, and Mrs T spends one day a week looking after her friend's baby while the mother does marriage guidance counselling, and it appears that children flock from miles away to the farm, so there can be fourteen sitting down to a meal at the weekend.

They also have a make-believe daughter of 13 (actually a miscarriage thirteen years ago) who sounded reasonably within their control, but said they are willing to foster a child of any age. Mrs Tolley would really like to have another baby of their own: 'I'm only forty—I suppose I could turn round and have another?', but their GP thinks this unwise; they imagine adoption would take too long to arrange and meanwhile Mrs T has considerable surplus energy. Marlshire is now in the position of needing foster-homes largely for short-stay children, adolescent girls on remand, and difficult adolescents committed to care—the last two categories are really more for professional-type foster-parents, and the high rates of payment would be hard to earn, but in view of the way they'd coped with Cathy (although I didn't meet her), giving her a secure framework and being able to alter their pattern to fit in with her, I think they seem to have potentialities.

Mrs Tolley wanted me to see round the house, which had been in a broken-down, rat-ridden state when they took it and which is now attractive. I asked her (half out of interest, half wondering if she'd be able to see similar scope in an initially unrewarding foster-child) if it had been disheartening to find the house like that, or had she been able to imagine it as it could be? She replied that she could always remember everything in any room once

41

she'd seen it, and could foresee it redecorated and refurnished. 'I'm very noticeable like that', she concluded, which amused me, as her girth must literally equal her height. I'm going there again in June.

24 May

I spent most of the morning writing pages of a more official version of the above Tolley family. Miss Farrar thinks it might be just the thing for a difficult 12-year-old girl of another fieldworker in this team, Mrs Marren.

P.m. Two visits in Marlford, to two addresses of Jimmy's mother given on his birth certificate. (a) his mother's previous address over ten years ago. I called at the house and told the woman I had a strange request . . . she'd only been there for six years, but told me what she could of the previous tenant who'd died six years ago—otherwise she knew nothing, but was intrigued. (b) an address in a street which is now being pulled down. The number I wanted is now taken over by a shop, but I learnt from a man in the road that (ironically) it used to be a Mother and Baby Home, now moved round the corner. So I went there, but the Matron was out and her assistant couldn't find any old records. A woman doctor called simultaneously to borrow cups, etc., for a Moral Welfare tea-party nearby, and told me that the Secretary of this Home might be there and be able to remember details of Jimmy's mother. So next thing I found myself at this Moral Welfare do in the vicarage, but the Secretary wasn't there.

Then I went on to Drayton to see Mrs Almond—I don't make appointments and called twice but she was out both times. It is just a week since Mr Tasker had his lengthy interview with her. The fruit-squash man called while we were there but she was too het up to see him then. Today she'd left a note for him on the door: 'Sorry about last week but I had a very important visitor and they could only give me a few minutes'—actually nearly one and a half hours, which only goes to show how differently time may pass for individuals in the same situation.

25 May

A.m. I phoned the Matron of the Mother and Baby Home—she has no records going back ten years ago, which seems odd for such a Home. Miss Farrar and I had a supervision session—looking backward and forward (I'm going away now until mid-June for exams in Barchester, followed by holiday). I'm doing a social history for George, and finishing generally—things seem to have drawn together conveniently for a pause.

P.m. Two interviews in Drayton.

First, a short one with Mrs Almond, just to tell her I'll be off for two and a half weeks. This was entirely different from previous interviews, perhaps partly because I'm now able to meet her on a more realistic basis—it was more of a conversation, less of a monologue. She recounted the latest incident of Eamon and his mother but we concentrated mainly on our own relationship. She gave me two indirect openings which I took up by asking if she finds my visits 'trying'. She asked suspiciously why she should find them trying, and I said she might wonder why I was visiting so often but it's because it is a sticky patch and I have more time than usual but I'm not coming in a critical spirit. . . . She protested that she was only too glad and grateful for my help and interest: 'If I had thought otherwise, I'd very soon have asked you what you were about, not in any way to hurt you, of course, but I'm rather honest like that . . . .'

This is superficial no doubt, but it seems worth trying to re-assure her. She added that 'some people don't seem to realize how extremely difficult the situation is'; I said I think I do—which surely must carry a ring of truth. Mrs Almond went on to say that she knew something of the difficulties of fostering, because she had been a foster-child herself. She didn't enlarge, but this was the first time she'd mentioned it (if the records are anything to go by) in nearly twelve years of being visited, and we only knew definitely last week that she and her husband were divorced.

Another way she uses me is in her comparison of my work and hers (as midwife and foster-mother). Previously she's often treated me as a child, or unmarried mother, or has implied I'm hors de combat by not being a mother, but once, when Eamon showed interest in my work, she pointed out the similarities between mine and hers. Today she said wistfully that she wished she had my opportunities 'for driving round and helping people—it would have been my cup of tea'. I said, 'Haven't we said before that our work is similar?' 'Yes, but I think yours is greater.' She said she might be going away too for a few days before Whitsuntide. Where? Barchester!

I haven't described Mrs Almond before—I think she's getting on for 60, middle-sized, with signs of eczema and rheumatism on her hands. She doesn't quite sound her Rs. She must have been at her peak in the 1920s, and therefore not untypically retains a somewhat faded 1920s appearance. This time, for the first time, she didn't offer to shake hands when I left and it seemed a more natural parting. It's odd that not shaking hands should be an advance, but I feel that Mrs Almond's handshake goes right back to its primitive origins, connected with fear of weapons.

Then I went to see Eamon's headmaster at Drayton grammar school. We had an hour's discussion—chiefly useful to him (?) because he's anxious to understand the situation as it affects Eamon's school work. He's a bit like a stage headmaster—a cross between Alastair Sim and Alec Guinness in looks and manner, and has a habit of keeping his eyes mostly closed and suddenly opening them, which is disconcerting. You go on looking at where his eyes should be and are half-dazzled when they emerge without warning —a handy trick for schoolboys. He thought so hard I could nearly hear him tick—for example, as we looked at Eamon's last school report, I mentioned the 15 per cent for Religious Instruction— he pondered deeply and then said it might of course have something to do with the RC battle. He agreed that, while we don't want to influence Eamon to change from RCism, this extra pressure is too much for him to take without breaking out or down somewhere. He knows the RC priest and thought he could be appealed to on these lines; at least for a breathing space, and that Father O'Sullivan would agree 'to whatever is most expedient for Mother Church'. In fact the headmaster offered either to see the priest for me, or to see him with me. I felt I should see the priest separately, but I think it helpful that the headmaster has the same idea if he should later happen to discuss it too. He wants to help in any way he can, although he has difficulty in identifying Eamon—not surprisingly, if he doesn't keep his eyes open.

(I did an 'interim report' on these two interviews, with promise of full ones later, after a break for exams followed by holiday.)

13 June

There's nothing like a gap in time for feeling you know a place better. My in-tray contained quite a lot. I was particularly pleased to have a letter from Mrs Ethel Rock at Long Winkley. She'd just returned from convalescence after her hysterectomy, was feeling better, and Jenny had been well looked after by Mrs Gladys, so she and her husband were pleased with the arrangements. Miss Farrar had replied in my absence, saying I'd write or call on return. I didn't think there'd be a chance to call, and shall be glad to, and will perhaps see Mrs Gladys or Mrs Clara's husband on the tractor in passing.

9 a.m. Supervision—I'm continuing with the three basic foster-homes:

(1) Mrs Almond and Eamon. Miss Farrar is pleased by the turn things are taking, and thinks that 'the fact Mrs A hasn't uttered during your leave shows you've won her—you were completely vulnerable then so she could easily have asked for someone else—the fact she didn't shows you've got her under your thumb.' I think the fact she didn't perhaps shows she's less apprehensive of my thumb.

(2) Mr and Mrs Yates, George and Jimmy. There's a letter from the northern mental hospital to say they have no knowledge of Jimmy's mother. I'm to ask Mr Hebditch (our expert on law, who administers all court work and adoption) whether sufficient effort has now been made to trace Jimmy's mother in order that her consent may be dispensed with, and then go ahead. Begin to work on George's relationship with his mother.

(3) Mr and Mrs Bateson, with David (adopted) and Sally (aged 5, physically and mentally handicapped). We agreed there seems less to do here at present, so my main aim is the observation of such a child.

(4) Continue to visit the prospective foster-parents, Mr and Mrs Tolley, with a view to Carol (aged 12, committed to care, now at Redlands reception centre) going there if approved at Redlands case conference on Thursday. Read Carol's file. The ten pages I wrote on the Tolleys' application are lost—hardly surprising when papers are moving in all directions to be seen, initialled and passed on. The system seems simple to an old hand, but as a student you feel very separated from your files. The others can

work for weeks without touching their files. They put papers in their out-trays marked with the file number, which are filed by Mr Parfit in the filing room. I keep my files on my desk and watch for papers returning and file them quickly myself like a broody hen. No doubt I'd get over this in time, but at first it feels like working in a vacuum, and files are less coherent if forms aren't filed in date-order.

New work:

(5) Adoption welfare supervision—a baby of $2\frac{1}{2}$ months, Carmen, with Mr and Mrs Hicks in Andersham.

(6) A tracing-plus job for a Scottish department, Cameronshire. Mr McTavish has left his wife and children there (plus two older boys by his first wife with their paternal grandmother)—one of the most involved families I've come across; everybody in the picture seems to have married twice and Mr McTavish (working in Marlshire as a woodcutter) is doing a rapid series of disappearing tricks. Cameronshire gives three addresses where he has been and left.

(7) Two coloured boys, Gregory and Joe, with a coloured foster-mother, Mrs Victor. Marlshire County is the 'care authority' (i.e. basically responsible) but the Marlford City Children's Department is the 'supervising authority' of its own foster-home. This is a temporary job for me because Gregory has asked to see his mother, now married. I'm to ask permission from Marlford City, meet the boys and Mrs Victor, meet the mother, and try to arrange a meeting between them. Being Miss Farrar, she foresees that the younger boy, Joe, will ask to see his mother too (also miles away in the depths of Marlshire). This mother is likely to be even less willing, but Miss Farrar says she may as well face it now under controlled conditions. Otherwise, when Joe is 18, she may 'be shocked suddenly to find a big, black man on her doorstep'. (This is partly in preparation for my employment in Loamshire where there is a bigger coloured population.)

(8) Guardian ad litem in an application from a mother and her husband to adopt Frances, aged 10. I'm to do this entirely with Mr Hebditch, our court officer. It seems complex and apparently if he feels I'm not relying on him completely he may be tempted to take offence and leave me holding the baby in a south Marlshire court. This is 'experience in working with someone funny. You can tell by the look on his face and the way he teeters about on

his feet when he's turning funny.' So. It's all the more awesome in that Miss Farrar rarely speaks of colleagues, or of other people at all, so candidly; she is mainly clear-cut on factual information.

I spent the rest of the morning seeing various people in the office, and clearing up small things like missing medical forms. I thought I'd visit the old foster-homes quickly, so as to have a fairly clear field for the new work, some of which has to be started soon. The Marlford City CO is on leave, I find, so that is one chore less for this week.

P.m. Visited two foster-homes in Drayton.

First, Mrs Yates. She was out, but I met her in the town. She sat in my car, talking hard. I'd discussed the effect on George (aged 13) that their adopting Jimmy might have, and they've now changed their mind, and think it wiser not to consider adopting Jimmy, at least for a time. On the whole I agree, especially as Mrs Yates's health is uncertain and her capacity with adolescent boys, and she does seem to need the boarding-out allowance. (Miss Farrar is sorry Jimmy's mother is not fully traced and faced at this stage, because 'she is almost certain to turn up later', although at the moment she seems most elusive.)

We discussed several other things, including George's future at school and subsequent employment. As we talked, Jimmy came up the road from school, straddling the gutter, spitting as he went. He didn't see us until Mrs Yates hissed reproof from the car-window and reminded him to say 'good afternoon' to me. He spat once more, either to demonstrate the necessity or to show unconcern, and then began to tell me very earnestly about his recent trip to London with the school. Later George rode up on his bicycle and told me about his playing football for Marlshire schools. (When I recounted the spitting to the fieldworker who normally visits this foster-home, she seemed to think I should have done something about it. But I think it's a pity if you can't enjoy spitting when you're 10, as there's not much chance later on.)

Second, Mrs Almond and Eamon. He was having a day off school with sickness—in pyjamas watching TV under a blanket. Occasionally, when Mrs Almond 'went on', he disappeared altogether under the blanket. (I'm beginning to see that it's impossible to keep this diary anything like full, because so much is happening.) But the main new thing with Eamon is that his mother, Miss Murphy, who has held the same ward-maid job in Marlford for about eight years, has suddenly left it, and is a waitress now in Drayton—living with her sister, brother-in-law and her second son Shaun (with whom Eamon has a complex relationship too) near to Mrs Almond's home, so now she visits here most evenings. They seem to have taken this in their stride so far—Eamon talks of his mother with a pseudo-tolerant, detached superiority.

The evening Miss Murphy moved, her brother-in-law called at Mrs Almond's, accusing Eamon of stealing from their house. Miss Murphy turned up hot on his heels, very upset that his allegation should be made against her son. As both women for once felt alike in the situation (defensive of Eamon) and as Miss Murphy seems to need Mrs Almond's support, the two women seem at least temporarily a little closer together—i.e. pulling the same way. I just hope Miss M's sudden change of employment and lodgings doesn't show she's in for one of her spells of panic, when she is apt to take a series of uprooting actions. She may be working towards having Eamon and all her nearest relatives under one roof. Her living so near now would seem to heighten potentialities for good or ill. After reading my report Miss Farrar said, 'This is fine, but don't forget Mrs A *is* a devil, and don't let her lull you into a false sense of security'!

14 June

A.m. clearing up in the office.

In the afternoon I'd intended to come to grips with my new work, but was alone in the office, and had been given some telephone calls to make. (Yesterday there was a motor-bike accident in Drayton—although unknown to each other, the rider used to be in care, and one of those seriously injured is currently in our care. I had to ring the hospital, and a children's department on the south coast so they could inform the mother.) Another fieldworker rang in from outside with an emergency, wanting me to go on telephoning about it, and what with the number of other incoming calls, I never stopped. People rang up in all sorts of moods—tearful, angry, excited . . . and in the middle I had an office interview with an unsupported mother applying on the spur of the moment for her baby to be received into care.

In writing up these conversations, I finished my first pad of pink memo forms, and the last sheet was a freak green one, which didn't interest me. When Miss Gibbs returned at 4.30 I was glad to see her and handed over the messages, expecting and hoping she'd go into immediate action. But the thing which really gripped her attention was the freak green memo form—she must have seen many thousands of pink ones in her time here, and I think it turned her world upside-down for a moment.

15 June

A supervision session first. At 12 noon, I was to see Father O'Sullivan (who has a higher status than a mere parish priest). I had quite dreaded this and been anticipating it for a long time, but at last felt able to make a reasonable appeal to him. I felt confident in outlining the situation, and justified in asking for a breathing-space for Eamon from the RC church on the grounds that his attitude to it is bound up with the conflict between his mother and foster-mother, and that any extra pressure at this point is likely to have an adverse effect on him, but that I hope (in time, if the relationships between the three of them should improve) he may return to RCism. This to me seems the only way.

But Miss Farrar stunned me in supervision by saying, 'The miraculous outcome to all this would be for you to get Eamon back to the RC church before you leave at the end of August.' She asked me to think very seriously whether my 'personal faith' would allow me to accompany Eamon to the RC church on Sundays. As it happens, my 'personal faith' allows me to do almost anything I want, though I find the RC service busy, and am not burning to drive nearly fifty miles on a Sunday to do this. I agree it would please Miss Murphy, though she might be envious if I succeeded where she'd failed. Mrs Almond would be upset. However, the religious question is being used as a symbol of conflict, and I'm not convinced that solving the symbol eases the real situation.

The main thing is that Eamon made his decision *not* to attend some months ago when he found the conflict intolerable, and I think it very important to respect his decision. I think he'd feel that, if he gave in, when the real situation is virtually unchanged, he'd have lost his small measure of hard-won independence and was again at the mercy of his adults. I'm supposed to be a reliable figure to him, but I think it would seem a volte-face if I suddenly took this line. I agree one could look to this goal, but think the time limit much too short. Miss Farrar thinks he's already had a breather, but in fact he's been in suspense all this time, and the freedom can't start really unless Father O'Sullivan agrees. I argued a bit (though I've few words to debate with Miss Farrar unless on paper) because I'd just begun to see daylight until she introduced this very smelly red herring. A miracle would be essential to achieve her aim, but I don't see that one can expect a dramatic one, when it would be just as much a miracle (but a more natural, co-operative one) if the situation eased a little in a couple of years, with the requisite amount of supportive casework.

On the other hand, Miss Farrar is good for me, because of her consistent rule about the need for everybody to *face* things. I do sometimes, but otherwise prefer to watch and see what happens and move with the positive force that's in the situation. You need to be very strong to face every contingency, and some clients might be stronger than I fear, but it can be devastating, so one would sometimes owe them more supportive time than one has to give. In another way, it is respecting the client to believe him capable of facing distress. But this situation is so changeable and explosive that I don't feel capable of doing anything except in my own way, and that slowly. Miss Farrar did say finally that, if I couldn't cope with Father O'Sullivan, I could always refer him to Mr Tasker.

On the way there I called at the third basic foster-home, the Batesons with Sally—all plain sailing at the moment. I arrived at the Presbytery as the Church clock struck 12 (which impressed him) with a mind so open as to be almost blank, feeling that things were far beyond my control—a state which is useful to me sometimes. Fr O'Sullivan is Irish of course, with what's known as hooded eyes, and he called me 'Child' throughout, which I quite liked, taking it in the spirit in which it seemed to be intended. I might have been more tactful if we'd discussed from the word go, but he left it entirely to me to begin. So I outlined the situation and made my appeal for a breather. He was quite hurt that I'd made it explicit that he was capable of exerting pressure;

I felt conscious-stricken and tried to soften it, but in view of what happened later I needn't have worried.

He assured me within minutes that not only was he in no position to exert pressure but that he certainly will not, now or in future. In fact he's given up hope of Eamon ever returning. 'There's a disintegrated boy if ever I saw one.' He was quick to grasp the gist, but blames Mrs Almond, thinking her 'possessive and wanting the boy body and soul'. I said I think she hasn't deliberately influenced Eamon against his religion, but this was the outcome of her relationship with Miss Murphy. We agreed Eamon is the most important, but he thought I should 'work on' Mrs Almond. He thinks I should tell her she's possessive, and that she has sinned against God and Miss Murphy by not bringing him up in the faith his mother wished, and by turning him against his mother.

Fr O'Sullivan said any child can be moulded, and he himself could turn any child he reared into a Hindu or Bush Baptist or anything he chose. He imagined it would 'break Mrs Almond's heart' if Eamon were removed, and that she has great pride in being a good foster-mother. I readily agreed, but then found he wanted me to use this in threatening Mrs Almond, even though he knows we have little statutory power. I said Mrs Almond is more than threatened enough already; that it's not for me to tell her she's sinned against God or Miss Murphy, and implied that it is not even expedient to threaten her, let alone anything else. He proceeded to act the interview he thought I should have with Mrs A.

This was quite extraordinary: he acted both parts—*me* (powerful, accusing, implacable) and *Mrs Almond* (very nervous, voluble and on the defensive). Mrs A grew to a crescendo of protesting distress but I remained tough and immovable, and gradually she became butter in my hands, admitted she had sinned, and promised to do better in future. I sat riveted, finding it both fascinating and distasteful. By the end, he was more convinced by his display than I. I told him he didn't really know Mrs A; that shattering her wouldn't react well on Eamon; that the only way I see is gradually to help her to feel a little differently, which is what I'm trying to do. He seemed to accept this, and was good enough, having told me how to tackle Mrs A, to ask me whether there was anything I think he should try to put across to Miss

Murphy if he should have further opportunities to discuss it with her.

I could only say that it seems valuable to treat her as a real mother, but not to encourage her to stand on her maternal rights as she hasn't been able to give him the other side in terms of care. We talked about Miss Murphy for a bit. (There is a widespread tendency, if A and B have got across each other, and A is obviously wrong, to think automatically that B must be right. People tend to do this here, by thinking Miss M would be a better person to have sole care of Eamon. But I don't.) There was a lot more than this, because we went ding-dong for an hour. Considering the interview was between an RC priest and me, it was surprisingly passionate, and we got on better than it may sound. Towards the end he said quietly that it seemed the two women are jealous. I said, 'And you know what jealous women can be like!' The full force of this suddenly seemed to hit him, because he leapt in his chair, struck his hands together and exclaimed with great feeling: 'Boys O boys! Jealous women!' We gathered any constructive ideas we had together, and I left quite pleasantly at 1 p.m.

To my surprise, Miss Farrar read my slightly toned-down report of this interview later in the afternoon 'with great enjoyment'. I rang Eamon's headmaster, really in the hope that he wouldn't now make a second, embarrassing suggestion to Father O'Sullivan about exerting pressure. The headmaster was glad to know, but asked was I sure that 'Father O'Sullivan's minions weren't putting pressure?' Next I shall see Eamon and Mrs Almond again to tell them the news; Miss Farrar says I should so tell Miss Murphy. I feel diffident about seeing Miss M because I'm afraid it has the effect of making her react wildly just to show who's boss, but as usual we are all to face it.

I spent the afternoon in the office, writing reports and letters, reading files. Thinking it high time to start some of the new work, I decided at 5.30 to go back to my lodgings and take my 'landlady' (actually the mother of a tutor to another course at Barchester) as navigator and moral supporter on a jaunt-cum-tracing-expedition. We started in far south-west Marlshire on the first two of the three addresses given by Cameronshire for finding the Scottish woodcutter: (a) in the wilds beyond Rickerton—he left there over three months ago, (b) a pub in South Folderton—he left over two months ago. Plot thickening.

16 June

A.m. worked in the office. During the morning I visited the third address—a snack-bar-cum-lodging-house in Marlford City. It was closed, but I nodded and becked at the owner through the glass door till she let me in, and proved quite informative. Mr McTavish left six weeks ago, and begins to sound a desperate character. His workmate, Tom, still visits her and she learnt a day or two ago from Tom that Mr McTavish is on a caravan site at Southerby, with 'wife' and one child. He and Tom work miles away, so one would only find them in at night. Several people are searching for him—mostly those to whom he owes money.

All I have to do is (a) find him, (b) tell him he could be prosecuted for failure to maintain his four children, (c) ask him for his consent to his first wife having custody of the two older children. I thought at this point that, as I'm genuinely quite busy now, perhaps I could work through Tom and the woman at the snackbar who wants to help. I could do it quite simply and effectively without stirring from Marlford City—but, I might have known, I'm to 'face it'. He may be watery-eyed with a stammer if and when I do catch up with him, but at the moment I imagine either all the searchers arriving en masse at the caravan like the last chapter of a thriller, or me threading my way through the caravan site by dim moon-light and the Scottish woodcutter lurking with his axe, like the first chapters ditto.

At 12.30 (until 7.30) I went with Miss Farrar to Redlands for their case conference plus Mr Tasker, all the fieldworkers with children in the reception centre, and relevant probation officers, headteachers, *et al*. There was a visitor from Cwmbachshire—I learned she virtually is Cwmbachshire, it being so unpopulated that she is the single children's officer/probation officer/moral welfare worker, etc., all rolled into one large woman. All the children currently in Redlands were discussed, and notes taken to record contributions on each one semi-verbatim. In particular we discussed Carol, and it was agreed that we should try to place her with my prospective foster-parents, Mr and Mrs Tolley, asking them if they'd like to undertake this job for two or three years of Carol's committal. (My report on the Tolleys, which was 'lost', reappeared just in time.)

17 June

In the morning, we started with a supervision session: I've had three this week, in preparation for Miss Farrar being away on leave for two weeks. In particular, we discussed the next stage with Carol, and how to see whether untried foster-parents are likely to cope with the range of behaviour problems exhibited by disturbed foster-children. For example: 'Find out if Mrs Tolley thinks her husband would mind if Carol soils at the breakfast-table. . . .' 'But she doesn't in fact soil, does she?', I ask, thinking Carol's many other problems plenty to be going on with. 'No, but find out their reactions.'

I'd planned a comfortably full day's work for today (Friday) and had made an appointment to see Carmen and Mrs Hicks (adoption welfare supervision). I'd also heard a rumour that I was to be given another application for care, but as nobody sounded urgent I gathered there was plenty of time. I went back to my desk at 10.30 and found the memo sitting blandly there about this case (message from the police the previous afternoon) and saw it was an emergency: the Hopgood family, well-known in the past; Mrs Hopgood deserted two days ago; three children— Keith (6), Sam (4½), Karen (14 months); Mr Hopgood on day and night shifts alternate weeks, something to be done by Sunday. I gathered I could go and explore the situation, ring up from Rickerton and ask permission to receive the children into care if necessary, fix up with any of three possible foster-homes in Rickerton, arrange clothes and bedding, etc., and move the children.

I said to Miss Beckwith whose case it should have been (only she's very busy), 'I had hoped to return to Barchester tonight for the weekend.' 'Oh,' she said, 'I thought you were working full-time now!' Instead of kicking her, I collected an RIC form, a bunch of Agreement forms and three medical forms, and went off at all speed; called at Andersham briefly to keep my appointment with Mrs Hicks (more later); went on to Rickerton to one housing estate, found Mr Hopgood had moved to his married sister's plus combined family on an estate the other side, and eventually had an interview with him.

Mr Hopgood's still in a state of shock. He has sore eyes, eye-lashes choked with matter, and a very hairy chest, including one straight hair about three inches long which caught my attention.

I found his sister was willing to keep his three children (over-crowded with her own two) for one week only. So Mr H and I filled in the RIC form and the three medical forms—he knew their birth-weights and some early milestones. Then I persuaded his sister to keep the youngest child, Karen, at least. Mr Hopgood doesn't want his wife back—she's gone off with another man and is reported as missing. We made what plans we could—he seemed, naturally enough, unable to look far ahead. I returned to the office, discussed with Miss Gibbs—it's going to be more complicated than I thought.

Next, a short talk with Miss Farrar and Miss Gibbs, so that the latter would know what I'm doing in the next fortnight. Another small complication—the guardian ad litem case. I've been seeing Mr Hebditch (court officer) about it and have been so careful with him in case he 'turns funny' that he'd insisted on accompanying me some distance next Monday evening for the home visit. I told him I'd manage with his help in between but we finally fixed to go together. I had a feeling Miss Farrar wouldn't approve, and mentioned it lightly to her today. She told him I must go alone, and we faced the risk of upsetting him. He seems to have taken it quite well.

During the rest of the afternoon I wrote reports, etc., and dictated two letters as from Mr Tasker (which is common pro-cedure for letters of any importance) to (a) the Hassex Children's Officer, near London, about Mrs Hopgood who hails from there; and (b) to Cameronshire telling their CO how far 'my social worker' (i.e. me) has got in tracing Mr McTavish and how she hopes to face him next week and will send a further instalment.

5.25 p.m. Heard a suggestion of my being given another case.

5.30 p.m. Said goodbye and left hurriedly for Barchester (seventy miles).

Miss Farrar thinks 'it's 90 per cent of the battle' to get the sort of reactions from people that I sometimes seem to get. I wonder if there's more to it, but said weakly that this was encouraging anyway. To enlarge: People can roughly be classified in various ways, including the way they cope in a new situation:

(1) Immediately impress their own personality on the new environment.

(2) Keep quiet (like the Yorkshire motto—'see all, hear all, say nowt') until they discover what's going on and how they can fit in.

(3) Follow a happy medium.

If one comes in group (2), one tends to get no reaction from very civilized, controlled people, and a variety of reactions from those less controlled according to their mood. In other words, if you can't find a happy medium yourself, it hinders other people from finding their own path. A character in a book I'm reading describes himself as 'a militant pacifist'—a static paradox is nonsense but one which moves flexibly over a period of time does seem to provide some solution.

20 June

A.m. odd jobs in the office. There was a letter from Cameronshire, crossing with ours, which rather steals my thunder. I was going to look for the McTavish caravan this morning, but the new letter gave the exact address very near where I'd thought, so I needn't have done the detective work last week. Also the nature of the mission has changed—it is now a question of asking them to confirm verbally their intention to have the two older boys (by the first wife) as soon as they can get a house, and urge them to do so soon.

I did find and talk with Mrs McTavish (the real second wife, apparently) peacefully, and got confirmation from her. It is still difficult to meet Mr McT—he is working in west Marlshire and returns only for short weekends. She and I arranged either that he'd call at the Marlford office on Saturday morning, or she will find out from him his working address and I will visit him there next week. My seniors are against his coming in to Marlford on Saturday (I don't think he'll come anyway) but I feel he will be off again if not seen soon, and a verbal confirmation completes the job Cameronshire asked us to do so far. I suppose it may impede his 'casework relationship' with me if he sees a colleague first, but he seems almost too fully occupied to have much of one, and the way I've had to track him down doesn't promise very well anyway. If Cameronshire wants more, I visualize working with Mrs McTavish, who looks too stolid to be very mobile.

P.m. East area Sub-committee. A financial item of mine was first on the agenda—I was expecting to have to agree that it was slightly unreasonable and that it'd gone through too quickly because of my inexperience, but the committee approved without delving. There was one sticky patch later, and Captain Shaw-Cooper who was so keen on the subjects of 'public money' and punishment at my first meeting continues in the same vein. Afterwards the fieldstaff and Mr Tasker had our usual cup of tea together at a café round the corner.

After that I had an hour's discussion with Mr Tasker at his request. He had read the report of my interview with Father O'Sullivan and sent a message to say he found it interesting and wished to talk further. I had no idea of department policy over RC priests so wasn't sure how he'd taken it, but it seemed he found it hard to believe. He asked me if I was really sure Fr O'Sullivan had said what he did; and then whether I thought I'd written objectively. I said I tend to write better than I speak, but that the report is accurate within the usual limits. I only realize in retrospect that he must have half-suspected I'd concocted a false report. Eventually he said wistfully that his own interviews with RC priests usually end in his being 'excommunicated', but that he supposed his age, sex, position and unsuitability for being called 'Child' made it more difficult for him to get on with them (I wasn't quick enough to reply that these very same factors made it easier for him than myself to get on with Mrs Almond, so he can't have it both ways). We discussed the whole situation again and seem to see eye-to-eye over it. He has taken an interest since meeting Mrs Almond.

In the evening I went to Finleigh, over twenty-five isolated miles away, in order to meet the mother, her husband (Mr Stokes), illegitimate daughter Frances aged 10, and two younger children of the marriage, in the guardian ad litem case for an 'own child adoption'. I thought them a very pleasant family but was there mainly to obtain endless information on four sides of two long foolscap sheets, with the aim of protecting Frances's interests as a representative of the court. Mrs Stokes had saved a question for me: whom should she tackle to get water laid on? At present it's well-water which must be boiled. I said I'd 'think', and let her know when I see her in court on 8 July.

21 June

A.m. in the office—completing forms, guardian ad litem report (approved by Mr Hebditch), letters, telephoning, etc. I've received Marlford City's permission to go ahead with the coloured boys, Gregory and Joe, and discussed Carol with her social worker Mrs Marren plus Carol's prospects with my prospective Tolleys. I also discussed one or two things with Miss Gibbs, my foster-supervisor. Occasionally she asks abrupt questions but seemed this morning just as surprised as I am, on getting a snappy answer. For example, on the guardian ad litem case:

'Does Frances *want* to be adopted by them?'

'Yes.'

'How do you *know*?'

'Because I asked her and she said so.'

P.m. my second visit to the Tolleys, to put the proposition of Carol as a tough job for a couple of years of her committal before she, we hope, returns home. We discussed Carol's stealing, epileptic fits, swearing, untidiness, her need of her own family (but not her imaginary 'soiling at the breakfast-table'), the possible reactions between Carol and various members of their household, working with the department, the general plan and so on.

Mrs Tolley very much wants to try, and seems capable to me. She was under less pressure than last time when she was completely prospective. We talked about other things, including haymaking and milk-prices, and her experience of difficulties with other children. She had a friend's toddler there by himself for a few days, who seemed thoroughly settled. She is experienced in the actual handling of children, but eager to compare ideas with me. I think her ideas are genuinely what she believes because she has a social worker friend whom she might expect to think as I do, but she tells me straightaway where she and her friend disagree—e.g. her friend doesn't hold with saying no to a child. Her ideas are simple, shrewd and flexible, and she examined any new thoughts carefully before accepting them. We left it (Mr Tolley being out) that I'd ring up next week, and possibly visit with Carol and Mrs Marren. If I visit too often, my car will depreciate rapidly what with the difficult journey and the way it literally hops down the farm-track.

I went on to Mr Hopgood in Rickerton—the emergency of last weekend looks like repeating itself this weekend. I thought it lucky to get a week's grace initially and to persuade his sister to keep Karen, the baby, and I felt quite clear that Keith and Sam would come into care this next weekend. But Miss Gibbs told me to tell him we couldn't help (unless very temporarily, but not to say so). Instead I was to ask him:

(a) His long-term plans (I felt unable to ask last time with his wife just gone, and anyway he can't know yet).

(b) Tell him he wouldn't be allowed to keep his council house unless he had his children there.

(c) Could he change his job?

(d) Or change his work shifts (i.e. come off night shifts, and let his sister have the children by day, and he return to the other side of Rickerton with them each night)?

(e) Could the children go to either of his wife's sisters living in London and Leeds?

(f) May I see his mother and ask her to give up her housekeeping job in order to keep house for him?

(g) Or could he employ a housekeeper?

(h) Not advisable, but could he stop work, go on supplementary benefits and look after the children himself at home?

He stood in front of me (sitting) while I put this series of doubtful propositions, as though he were on the carpet, and I didn't ask him to sit down in his territory because he was free to do so and it was no good pretending we were having a cosy chat. He was looking after his three children and his sister's two while she rushed out to the shops—and what with the trying behaviour of the children, and the extreme heat, and the fact that he'd just got in from a long day's work and hadn't had a meal, and my string of impertinent questions, I quite expected him to lose his temper, but he didn't. In the end I pushed him into asking his mother to keep house for him (she's over 60 with high blood pressure) and to ask his employers (whom he dreads) if he can come off night shifts. I said I'd see his mother too and come back on Thursday.

I see the need for this sort of interview and don't think children should lightly be received into care, but it makes the job more exacting to waste time haggling in this way when you know that by the weekend you'll either have left the family in an impossible situation or will have a hell of a rush getting them fixed up.

I made two attempts to see his mother afterwards without success.

22 June

A.m. in the office, writing up yesterday's interviews, letters, etc. A Rickerton health visitor rang up about the Hopgood family. She's very worried. Apparently Mr H has had a bad time with his wife recently. (On reading the thick files more thoroughly, I find she is ex-approved school, he drinks heavily and has been on probation after attempted suicide, and that the boys' behaviour is very disturbed, partly through frequent separations from their parents.)

I wrote my report of yesterday's interview with Mr Hopgood, quite dispassionately, and gave it to Miss Gibbs without saying, 'For God's sake, relent!' She came over to talk, and said to my relief that it looked as though the two boys would have to come into care, so I could look for foster-homes this afternoon without telling Mr Hopgood yet. She went on to discuss the whole question of her responsibility for deciding whether children should come into care, and how she feels quite different when she actually meets the families concerned. We were mutually sympathetic and concluded it's tough on all parties. I think the other fieldworkers, in the same boat as me, had been on to her yesterday, and Miss Beckwith surprised Mr Tasker by telling him the 1948 Act was out of date.

I was just thinking what a long way away my first short-stay case seemed and how that had different complexities, when Inspector Worth (NSPCC) rang me up about the Chubbs. I hadn't expected them to crop up again until Mrs Chubb had time to have another baby. Mr Worth had a long story—Mrs C is still living with the handicapped 18-year-old youth and another 'friend of his' in the house; the state of the garden is enough to cause eviction, the house and bedding 'disgracefully filthy', the children dirty and neglected, and Mrs Chubb will keep going to the ferry with all the children to help her man run the ferry, and sometimes they all sleep there. The police are about to pounce with Place of Safety Orders unless Inspector Worth can stave them off, and he will keep me informed.

P.m. went to Rickerton. First, to see Mr Hopgood's mother. I still couldn't find her at home, but was at the wrong house yesterday! Second, to find a foster-home for Keith and Sam. Miss Beckwith, whose patch it is, had given me suggestions of four sets of foster-parents, mostly able to take one child. I went to the first, on the same housing estate as the Hopgoods' basic home, and Mrs Chapel very soon agreed to have both boys if necessary. This means she'll have five boys in the house, and will have to alter her working hours to fit in with her husband's duty-times, but she'd manage she said. We made all the necessary arrangements including rubber sheets and a preliminary visit tomorrow. I felt better, and left work half an hour early, being not far from my lodgings by then.

(The rumour of another case turns out to be an adoption selection plus potential supervision later. I was also offered another case today, from Ireland—it's to report to a court there on 29 June for an Interim Adoption Order and to continue with welfare supervision until the family returns to Ireland in September (husband in the Army). I turned this offer down, as I haven't enough evenings left to complete a report before 29 June. My seniors begin to seem keen to have me working at the weekend, and I've agreed to do a Saturday morning duty in mid-July, when I shall be in Marlshire anyway, in the hope that they will then ease off. They may think a student isn't broken in until she has this discipline, but if they only knew I'm long past it and out the other side, and don't intend to work such ridiculous hours in future as in my previous job.)

23 June

A.m. couple of hours' work in the office.

10.45 visited Mrs Victor (coloured foster-mother in Marlford)—out. Went on to Drayton: Mrs Almond—out. Mrs Yates—out. Had lunch by the river, early. Went back to Mrs Almond—out. Back to Mrs Yates at 12.30—all the family at home. We've been trying to coax Mrs Yates to take George and Jimmy for their annual medical examination since January, and I went (under instruction) today to tell her tactfully that, if she didn't do it within a month, I'd take them myself. Mrs Yates took the wind out of my reluctant sails by saying she'd already fixed an appointment with her GP for next Monday. In Drayton, Mrs Almond specializes in confinements and Mrs Yates lays out corpses—both ends of the alphabet.

P.m. went back to Marlford; reached Mrs Victor's colourful home at 1.10. She talked to me till 3.00 p.m.! She belongs to

Marlford City, so I only went with their permission to see Gregory and Joe, and to discuss the beginning of the plan for them to meet their white mothers (coloured-soldier fathers long since returned to the USA). But I'm thankful to have met Mrs Victor (no husband now). She seems to be of pure West Indian blood, with grey bushy hair and white eyebrows—the first I've met with a perfect English accent, and a very wide vocabulary. She sees herself humbly as a real lady, and I could well see her as a world-famous personality—certainly a strong personality.

Recently I've met two people who acted: Father O'Sullivan, and now Mrs Victor. We sat on a sofa and she acted her experience with a large number of foster-children, particularly with Gregory (quiet and thoughtful) and Joe (quick-tempered and happy-go-lucky). A towel and swimming trunks suddenly hurtled through the open window against the plastic curtains and fell on the floor, followed by Joe through the door. She has six coloured foster-children at present, and there must be a rich flow of emotions according to what she acted. She takes white short-stay children too (I gathered indirectly—she's beyond colour). For example, the Marlford City worker arrives: 'Mrs Victor, I don't know what to do!' 'Why not?' 'I've got four children outside in the car. . . .' 'Bring them in!' 'I hoped you'd say that!'

It's now clear for me to write to Gregory's mother (married, miles away, whom he doesn't know). He has asked that she should meet Mrs Victor before she meets him. I imagine this is the way he's planned to introduce the colour question, and to show how impressive it can be. After meeting Mrs Victor, it's strange to me to realize that we shall have to tread carefully so as not to embarrass the white mothers and their unwitting white husbands.

3.10 p.m.—worked in the office.

4.00 p.m.—went to Rickerton. At last I found Mr Hopgood's mother. She told me she couldn't help as she's over 60 with high blood pressure and already has a gentle housekeeping job. She felt safe, having heard on the Rickerton grapevine that I was looking for foster-homes yesterday! She said her son has just heard from his wife, and that the whole thing was tragic, especially for the children.

Next I visited Mr Hopgood at his married sister's. He persists in standing in front of me while I sit, but looked much better today. Even the three-inch hair on his chest seems to have slipped back into place. We compared notes, and agreed to fall back on the fostering plan which is complex enough. I asked about his wife. Previously he was determined not to have her back. He heard from her this morning, asking if she could return. The man she went with has already returned. He has replied saying he is willing for her to come back. This means his very helpful sister has 'finished with him' (until the next crisis) and his mother also disapproves.

Mr Hopgood goes on night shift on Sunday, which is the last day his sister can help, and the day the children should be fostered. But will his wife return on Saturday, Sunday, next week or at all? And would Miss Gibbs, not to mention Mrs Chapel, agree to carry on with the fostering meanwhile? I nipped out to the nearest phone-box to speak to Miss Gibbs—she'd already left for a visit to a nearby small children's home. I went round there and caught her as she arrived, for a five-minute discussion. We decided:

(1) If Mrs Hopgood returns before Sunday morning, they'll all return to their own home, and Mr H will inform Mrs Chapel nearby.

(2) Proceed with the fostering plan to be on the safe side. Mr Hopgood will take the two boys there on Sunday morning if necessary.

(3) See if Mrs Chapel and Mr Hopgood are willing to make a private arrangement between themselves to save the official machinery churning into action if it's only for a few days.

(4) If Mrs H doesn't return soon, the children will in any case be received into care.

(5) If Mrs Hopgood does return, am I willing to continue visiting on a family casework basis, particularly with regard to the marriage? I said, 'I thought Marlshire didn't do preventive work?' 'There's no reason why you shouldn't if you think you've got time—otherwise refer it to Probation.' 'All right.'

I went back to Mr Hopgood (am getting quite fond of him) and we talked this over. He fitted in, and agreed to the private arrangement with Mrs Chapel with a little persuasion. I didn't intend to mention the possibility of my visiting him and his wife later on, until the next stage was reached, but found myself asking if he'd like this. Considering how I've had to push him around, I was surprised to hear him reply that, if he's to make a go of his marriage he will need to talk things over in future, but we'll wait to see if his wife wants visits too first. Then we put the boys' raincoats on for their introductory visit. I thanked his sister for her help—she was holding Karen, the baby, murmuring hypnotically to her, 'You call *me* mummy now, don't you? I'm your mummy now, aren't I?'—which isn't very helpful as the real mummy may be buying a return ticket at this moment.

As Mr Hopgood, Keith (6), Sam (4½) and I set off in my car, I was disturbed to realize that we'd had no chance to prepare them at all. I started explaining, 'We're just going to Mr and Mrs Chapel's home very near your own home, where you might be going to stay for a few days, or you might not, if. . . .' Mr Hopgood said despairingly, 'I don't think they'll understand.' And I gave up because it's really impossible to explain such protean plans to a child, when it all depends on whether or not their mother comes home. It was hard to see them a bit frozen, wondering what next. They've both been in care before and seem to know me (or my role) better than I know them. (On reading the files properly I see just how difficult these children have been to foster in the past, and said to Miss Gibbs, 'But it will all add to the interest, no doubt'—which startled her, but if she perceives my attitude as tough/cynical, she has less need herself to show me how it's done, and things go more smoothly! I have no qualms in exerting a little secret manipulation on tough women in authority over me. Although, when it comes to the crunch, you do get real support.)

We trailed into the foster-home hand-in-hand—Mr Hopgood unshaven in working-clothes, Keith and Sam scruffy with battle-scratched faces. The Chapels have a higher material standard than any Hopgood environment—Mrs C is quite polished, and her younger son in pyjamas had that incredibly clean look of a cared-for child ready for bed. Mr Chapel eased things by appearing in gardening clothes and struck, I thought, just the right note with Mr Hopgood. I explained the situation with Mr H's help (he is touchingly ingenuous about his wife) and I thought the Chapels wonderful in the way they grasped it naturally, and agreed to fit in with whatever happens over this weekend on a provisionally private basis.

We rehearsed the various possibilities and the need to let Mrs Chapel know either way on Sunday morning. Mr H has signed an RIC form just in case, as he'll be a night-bird next week. I had a final word with him outside and last saw him, walking off to his own home round the corner, holding both boys' hands in the rain. I set off home. Ten minutes later, found I'd forgotten to give Mrs Chapel the rubber sheets and returned with them. It was as well to see her on her own to make sure she isn't overwhelmed—she's a fairly new foster-mother. I said I could call in on Sunday evening on my way back from Barchester, but am going on Monday morning.

24 June

I rang the health visitor in Rickerton to keep her in the Hopgood picture; then worked in the office most of today. We seem short-staffed—Miss Beckwith is on leave—and there were several near emergencies which died down to some extent. One good thing is that workers in other local agencies know our department policy and don't cry wolf. In the afternoon I went to see Mrs Almond again, but she was out for the third time this week, so I've tried, but am not sorry to let this group of sleeping dogs lie for a week. Miss Gibbs is briefed ready to see the Scottish woodcutter if he does turn up tomorrow (Saturday) morning. I wrote to Gregory's mother at her working address, putting his request to see her as gently as possible, though it's bound to be a shock—he is 16 years old now.

27 June

I arrived all set to get on with the Hopgoods, but Miss Gibbs seemed to have had a busy weekend and asked me to do two bits of work near Rickerton. She did see Mr McTavish for me when he called here on Saturday, and gave him some tips about finding a house as well as completing what Cameronshire required of us.

I went first to a remote village to see the foster-parents of Fay Locking (aged 4). Miss Beckwith received the five Locking children into care (while their mother is in hospital with mysterious, serious symptoms) just before her leave, and Fay's foster-home had broken down so that she had to be moved on here on Saturday. She is a coeliac child (new to me) and Miss Gibbs had spent Sunday trying to obtain gluten-free flour, which I delivered this morning, plus a diet sheet and a willingness to discuss the needs of such children (some gleaned from Miss Gibbs and the rest translated from other dietetic peculiarities). Fay, surrounded by toys, was sleeping off a post-breakfast temper-tantrum when I arrived, and the flour was welcome. The foster-father nipped in from his outdoor work and had an unusually maternal attitude, so it was like talking with two foster-mothers. They had only applied to foster on Friday, and were given Fay on Saturday! So they are rather enjoying this situation, which probably wouldn't have arisen if one of their relatives weren't fostering another of the Locking family.

At 11 a.m. I arrived at Mrs Chapel's to see whether or not she had Keith and Sam Hopgood. She'd had them for one day since 9.30 a.m. Sunday, and asked me very calmly to move them today as they were too difficult for her to manage. Last Thursday I was impressed by her unharassed acceptance of the uncertainties, but realize now she must appear calm at all costs. I'd tried to prepare her for difficult children, and it was assumed they'd be boarded-out although other foster-homes have broken down in the past. It's two years since they've been officially in care, so I wasn't sure how difficult they'd be now. Keith used to be obstreperous but has become quieter since starting school and I imagine more withdrawn, and Sam is the wild one now. He, like the younger Keith, doesn't understand 'No' so, whereas another child might show some variety in mischief, Sam shows mercurial persistence on a few set lines non-stop.

Part of Mrs Chapel's rejection, which I find harder to understand, seems to be connected with the boys' previous neglect. It seems she was disgraced not only by their being dirty and underfed, but because Keith has a bad bruise on his back where, he said last night in the bath, his father had kicked him. I feel responsible for this breakdown, which arises partly because I had insufficient knowledge of the parties concerned, having put my efforts last week into averting the need for care. I told Mrs Chapel I'd come back; went on to see Mr Hopgood, and knocked him up from sleeping after his night shift (no fun on a housing estate). He wasn't too pleased and has heard no more news of his wife. I explained I was sorry we'd have to move Keith and Sam—he wasn't surprised and isn't sorry perhaps to be relieved of them for a time.

I didn't do the other job for Miss Gibbs near Rickerton until Thursday, but went back to discuss the above with her. Apparently we are currently scraping the bottom of the foster-home barrel in

Marlshire; I was quite glad there were no alternatives to try because the more certain reception centre seems better at this point. I obtained permission from Mr Tasker and from Mrs Willcox at Redlands to move the boys there today. Mr Ripley, a fieldworker, was willing to act as escort in order to drive them forty miles more safely. From 4.00 to 5.30 I went between Mr Hopgood's home, his sister's and Mrs Chapel's making various arrangements. Mrs Chapel said she'd always be willing to foster again—'I enjoyed the good children I've had before, but. . . .' 'These aren't children!', her husband added.

Keith and Sam quite enjoyed the long journey during which we explained as much as we could, though they showed few reactions on leaving Rickerton or on arriving at Redlands. Sam seemed most distressed in wondering where my car was if I was travelling in Mr Ripley's car; also he was over-excited in expecting passing cars to crash. Staff and other children at Redlands seemed struck by the smallness of these two as they walked in across the large entrance hall. I told Mr and Mrs Willcox about them and they were just going to bed as we said goodbye.

28 June

Apart from completing forms for the above reception into care, social histories were needed for Redlands, and it took most of my spare time to do these. It's understandably difficult to sort out the history of an adolescent, but I wouldn't have expected the movements of two children aged 6 and $4\frac{1}{2}$ to be quite so complex. There are periods when the family is together, and other times of up to two years when they are spread out over Marlshire and Hassex. Mrs Hopgood does things like travelling up to Hassex, dumping a baby on her sister-in-law and vanishing, or posing as a 17-year-old girl living with her 18-year-old 'fiancé' while her children are in care.

In the afternoon, Mrs Marren and I went to Redlands to see Carol (aged 12) and discuss her possible placement with the Tolleys. I heard about Keith and Sam's first twenty-four hours here, and Sam's quota of mischief, and spoke to Sam briefly while he was playing skittles with his bodyguard. Carol cried when we told her about my prospective foster-home. She'd been hoping to go to the children's home in Rickerton, apparently feeling a home would represent less of a break with her real home; also although she's committed to care she must have been hoping against hope actually to go home now. Mrs Marren brought Carol's chair nearer hers and continued to attempt discussions. Much later, after Carol had cried herself out in the cloakroom, Mrs Marren talked again with her privately. We'd suggested visiting the Tolleys with her on Friday. Carol's own idea was that, if she had to be fostered, she'd like it to be done quickly (unfortunate Macbethian flavour) so would prefer to lengthen her first visit into a weekend. We agreed, if this was what she wanted.

29 June

A lot was happening in the office. In the afternoon I went to Withydean in west Marlshire, where I had an appointment with Mrs White (Gregory's mother) at 3 p.m. I'd received an enthusiastic letter from her, saying, 'I would very much like to meet Gregory.' I called for her at the hotel where she works, and she came out to sit and talk in the car. Considering that the whole thing is concerned with colour, she is strikingly colourless—small and slim, white overall, very fair hair and skin, only tried to make one original remark and forgot what she started to say. She greeted any suggestions I made with a whispered drawl, 'All right', though presumably she must be quite het up about meeting her son, and she is risking her husband finding out to some extent. However, we began to make plans, and she's willing to come by train to Marlford on her half-day to meet Gregory.

As it was too late to get back to the office by 5.30, I slipped over the border to the sea—Mrs Marren told me only yesterday that I hadn't lived, not having been there.

30 June

During part of the morning I made a fourth unsuccessful attempt to see Mrs Almond in Drayton, and left a written message.

At lunchtime, I took a pram to a foster-mother in a village beyond Rickerton. She has the baby, Dawn, of the Locking family, who has just had her routine medical examination, and the GP found a rare condition in which the two halves of the body develop at different rates. The foster-mother visualizes frequent visits to hospital, etc., so asked for a more easily-transportable pram. So in the Locking family there is this baby, a coeliac child, another deformed child, the mother mysteriously ill, and the father 'ever such a funny little man' who is walking miles now to keep in touch with his family. This foster-mother has invited him regularly for Sunday lunch. Dawn's condition is obvious (once you know)— her legs are a different length and the creases differently spaced. She is only six months old now, but will be lame later unless something can be done. Her foster-mother has a blunt sense of humour, and is unusual in taking an acute interest in the work of the whole department, so is very conscious of being part of a team although she lives in the wilds miles away from headquarters.

In the afternoon, I did the interview in Rickerton I meant to do last Monday. It was to assess the suitability of a great-aunt, Mrs Nash, to act as foster-mother for her 13-year-old niece now in London, and to send a report to the East Dowling London borough responsible for the care of Yvonne. Apparently in the past, Yvonne and her family were notorious here in Rickerton, and East Dowling (having coped at their end for a year or two) are now exhausting their resources, and banking on this young 'great-aunt' filling the future breach. It wasn't easy trying to form an opinion of Mrs Nash in one interview, but she is going to London on holiday soon and could be seen again there by the worker who knows Yvonne. I liked one slip of the great-aunt's: 'My father was headmaster of X (famous public school) for many years—I mean head gardener.'

At teatime I met Mrs Marren in Rickerton, and we went to see the Tolleys, prospective foster-parents for Carol. We thought we'd like to see them once more, as Carol is speeding things up, and I felt it high time that Mrs Marren met the Tolleys' for herself without merely relying upon my inexperienced impressions. The odd thing was that we found Mr Coombs there, having a cup of tea. We knew he'd just changed his job but not that he was delivering groceries to these out-of-the-way farms. He and his wife are in charge of the small Brayley Children's Home, where Carol nearly went and may still have to go. He didn't know we were visiting here about Carol, and Mrs Tolley didn't know his connection with us.

After he'd gone, we talked for ages, discussing Carol a second time. Mrs Tolley is becoming more natural and forgetting her pseudo-refinement to the extent where it is delicate to discuss Carol's 'problem of swearing'. Also she is now really thinking what it would mean to have Carol living here—previously she was just anxious to be acceptable as a new foster-parent. We made plans for our visit tomorrow with Carol. Mrs Marren didn't volunteer afterwards her impression of 'my' Tolleys—too soon for her to know yet, I suppose. My car seems to have done nearly 6,000 miles since starting in Marlshire.

I July

A.m. got up to date in the office.

12 noon: Mrs Marren arrived from Redlands reception centre with Carol, and we went on together to the Tolleys. It seemed that all parties were as prepared as possible—it just remained to see what happens on meeting. We spent the rest of the day there. Carol had lunch with the family in the farm-kitchen while Mrs Marren and I ate our sandwiches in the orchard. Then Mr Tolley returned to his hay-making and Mrs T and Carol rejoined us.

It never ceases (unjustifiably) to surprise me when people who are really very concerned with one thing that's on the spot (in this case Carol) concentrate because of their very concern on something trifling in comparison. In short, Mrs Tolley talked our hindlegs off, and we couldn't, or didn't, interrupt. She talked to me about farming, and gossiped charitably to Mrs Marren about everyone in the district, and eventually realized herself that we were 'going on like old apple women'. Meanwhile Carol was overcome by doubts and strangeness, and relapsed into sulks and then tears. Mrs Tolley and I (conscience-stricken both) talked it over in the kitchen, while Mrs Marren talked with Carol in the orchard. What helped most was the arrival of the questionable niece, Cathy aged 17, home from work. She seemed acceptable to Carol in a way which the rest of us weren't, temporarily, and soon the two of them were exploring the farm—so thoroughly that we couldn't find them when it became essential to leave.

Earlier Carol had wanted to call off her weekend visit but had become a little mollified, and Mrs Marren promised to collect her on Monday to go back to Redlands for a breather. We didn't like leaving without seeing Carol, but left messages, and Mrs Marren said she'd ring up during the evening. Mrs Tolley has several jaunts up her sleeve for the weekend, including a family picnic, so it's possible that Carol will have an entirely different picture by Monday. I hope so.

4 July

Miss Farrar is back—we had a short discussion just to see where I am. We decided I'd spend three days mid-week with three other students from the University of Collingham (who started last week in the other areas) when they come to headquarters here for a comprehensive teach-in.

A.m. went to see Mrs Victor to make the next bit of the plans for Gregory's mother to visit. Mrs Victor had lost her voice so I had a clear field for once, and we arranged 14 July, hoping her usual liveliness will have returned by then.

P.m. went to Mrs Almond's—out for the fifth time.

Then I called at the third basic foster-home: Mrs Bateson and Sally. This situation seems to run on quite happily, though I think there might be more if one started delving—for instance, Mrs Bateson said suddenly today that she often thinks 'it must be planned for some couples to be childless' so that they're free to care for deprived children. She is so attached to Sally that it's difficult to know whether she fully recognizes Sally's handicaps, though I think she is doing so a little more now Sally has started school. She thinks 'it must be terrible for Sally to have always to make such an effort to speak', and Sally has developed a habit of saying, 'Hum, hum . . .' to fill up the gaps between her uncertain flow of words. Mrs Bateson seems to enjoy Sally and the problems must be outweighed to some extent by Sally's pleasant temperament. Sally showed me some books of photographs of herself and her adopted 'brother' David earlier. She sat by me in the big armchair and noticed halfway through that she was crumpling my skirt, and straightened it before sitting down again. I thought she looked much more abnormal in the photographs and wonder whether it's because the camera emphasizes that sort of thing or whether her appearance is becoming more 'normal'.

Back to Mrs Almond's—out: note on the door—'Eamon. I'm over at the Cross. Come and meet me, Nana' (a few weeks ago I should have read her slightly off-key religiosity into this phrase!). So I parked outside and waited. Eventually they turned up, he darting on ahead and Mrs Almond in the rear, very respectable in white cotton gloves and a cardigan shrunk with frequent washing. She noticed me before Eamon, but I saw both of them first while I was quite unexpected, and was pleased and surprised that both their faces lit up as an immediate genuine reaction instead of clouding over involuntarily followed by polite smiles. As I suspected, Mrs A has a short-term nursing job which takes her out each day. She looked tired and I couldn't stay much longer so we talked outside.

Apparently things are going all right and Eamon 'is a different boy this term' though I seem to remember her saying that last term. He starts terminal exams today and she thinks (so do I) it'll be interesting to see how the results compare with last term's—which were so indicative of his disturbedness then. She expects an improvement, and will be satisfied with a small one. I asked how Miss Murphy is. The only difficulty at present, Mrs A says, is that she's 'playing up a little' as regards her weekly payments for Eamon since starting this new waitress job locally. We all know Miss M is 'a living rule' when it comes to making regular payments for her sons' private upkeep, so she must be feeling the pinch badly. Mrs A says she's dependent upon this income from Miss M, but daren't (I imagine) be too demanding lest Miss Murphy decides to move Eamon somewhere cheaper—perhaps under the same roof at her sister's where she lodges now. At the moment Mrs Almond shows no pressure of feeling about Miss M —previously she couldn't keep her tongue off her in her need to let off steam.

So it's worth recording that I think the situation is much improved just now. Somebody has said that you don't always notice when things are all right, which is fair enough ordinarily, but I think a social worker should have the benefit of recognizing these short periods because the clients certainly don't make a point of telling you (perhaps thinking we're only interested in trouble!) and breathers might otherwise pass as the uneasy peace between crises. After a bit Eamon came outside to talk too— about his exams and swimming and summer holidays soon, and was wanting to know my opinion about a TV programme 'which proved that a sample of boys were more concerned with *things*, and the girls with *people*'. He was more friendly than he's been before— earlier I've felt to get on quite well with him sometimes, but he had an understandable defence in a manner scrupulously polite towards grown-ups and slightly supercilious.

He suddenly put his head through the car window, and said in a charming, confidential way, 'I say, Miss Sparrow, 'd'you like a cup of tea?' I couldn't refuse, so followed him in, with Mrs A asking me to take her as I found her as she hasn't much time for housework at present. Eamon took trouble in making a good cup of tea and was pleased to be complimented. When I started to tell them I'd seen Father O'Sullivan, they both listened closely. I said Fr O'Sullivan seemed to understand; that of course he'd like Eamon to go back to the RC church but wasn't going to worry him about it. Eamon appeared greatly relieved. Mrs Almond said, 'I'm so glad Father O'Sullivan's come round to it at last', and proceeded to make a little speech about Eamon 'now being free to look into his heart'. I agreed more or less, and tried to reinforce the fact that Eamon's new-found freedom includes freedom to return to RCism if and when he feels so inclined. He looked a bit sheepish and nodded vaguely. I left it there, as my previous work was directed towards decreasing the conflicting pressures put on him by his adults. Mrs Almond went on to tell me about a girl in her care many years ago who is now engaged, and repeated the speeches of homely advice she'd given to mother and daughter. Eamon tended to disappear while this was going on, and may become quite impatient over this sort of thing soon.

The situation has time to blow up once or twice more before I leave, but I don't think one can hope for much more than its present state. Whatever Mrs Almond lacks, she has got staying-power and I don't see her changing much without a major work of reconstruction, and I imagine she'll be small beer once re-incorporated into Mrs Garvey's caseload. Whether her trite sentimental phrases are rooted in her or added through tribulation, I don't think that a person who can bear to use them, or enjoy using them or hide behind them, is likely to come very far into the open without breaking down. She and Eamon seem happy in each other's company, and I feel that his affection for her is more natural and genuine than hers for him, so I don't think it does him any harm to love her, whether she's a sick person or 'a devil' or what. It's impossible to tell any of the characters here what to do, so the choice lies between removing Eamon forcibly to a healthier form of care, trying to make drastic changes subtly in

Mrs A and Miss M and redesign them into 'fit persons', or trying to maintain things with gradual easement showing through the usual ups and downs—I plump for the latter, while remaining open to further opportunities, which *is* 'casework', however it's defined.

When I left, Eamon went to open my car door, while Mrs Almond (not such a good sign?) squeezed my hand without scratching and whispered, 'You're a dear!'—her face all creased with emotion. They both waved till I turned the corner.

5 July

I wrote up interviews, etc., in between-whiles. The three students from Collingham University arrived for our three-day teach-in—I've met one of them before, and another knows one of my fellow-students. Our programme began at 11 a.m. with an introductory talk by Mr Tasker and Miss Farrar—really more meaningful to me at this stage than it would have been at the beginning. There is still a questioning note, not entirely misplaced, about any 'authoritarian element' there may or may not be in the set-up. It may be justified if senior officers are willing to take final responsibility over years of experience, because junior fieldstaff don't always stay very long, and some people do tend to turn things upside-down and then press on to pastures new. The danger (apart from their silver lining) of reformers seems to lie in their energy for destruction which sometimes wanes during the slower process of building things up again.

12.30. we all went to the local social workers' lunch club for two rather overwhelming talks about nuclear disarmament. The programme after 2 p.m. was following a CHA form round the office with Mr Tasker—I'd done this before so got on with other work.

3.30 p.m. the person in administrative charge of all the various residential homes and centres discussed the running of them.

5.15 p.m. Mrs Marren, Miss Farrar, Miss Gibbs and I discussed together whether Carol should go to live with the Tolleys. The verdict on the introductory weekend was that Mr and Mrs Tolley want Carol, in spite of the difficulties which may or may not have registered properly even though they've been told at least three times.

Carol is not so keen although she'd had an artificially happy weekend (i.e. an unusual number of outings). She isn't exactly against going to live there, but still vaguely hankers after the children's home—in an attempt, one imagines, to play for time before leaving Redlands (which she's accustomed to) and still having wild hopes about going home. Redlands' staff consider her ripe for leaving there, and that she could well be an agitator in a small children's home environment. At this point, we ourselves decided for Carol: that she should try the Tolley foster-home. Had it been plainer sailing, I might have continued by supervising Carol there until I leave. But it's obviously more important for Carol to be helped to settle down there by someone she already knows and likes—so Mrs Marren is carrying on, and I might visit later to say goodbye.

General plan: Mrs Marren will visit the Tolleys this week with Carol's mother. Carol will probably go there next week, in order to start school in Rickerton before the long holidays, and will have a weekend at home before the end of term; followed by short holidays at home during a possible two-year period, and then return home for good if she and her family grow more able to cope in the meantime.

6 July

9–10.30 Miss Gibbs talked to the four of us about applications for reception into care—an interesting discussion, as she asked for our reactions to a number of really knotty problems. When listening to the most fruity of these, it's almost incredible what tangled webs some families get themselves tied up in with added complexities when measured against the functions of the so-called welfare state and the rights of rate-payers. . . .

10.45–12.30 Mr Hebditch on administering adoption procedure, and the fieldworker's role in court. Left us breathless.

2–3.00 p.m. Miss Gibbs on child protection (i.e. private foster-care) and other peripheral activities—again discussed interesting cases.

3–4.00 p.m. The senior administrator, Mrs Burke, on HO records and area sub-committees—she managed to enthuse us over the statistics, especially when related to various local authorities.

4.15–5.15 p.m. Miss Gibbs on operational research. She has

worked on about twenty-seven subjects; the latest is fieldworkers' caseloads—an average of nearly a hundred a decade ago, and about fifty cases per worker now (frills such as the Scottish wood-cutter would not count).

More telephone calls about Carol—I hear she is quite expecting to go to the Tolley foster-home, which is just as well. Mrs Tolley is pleased and suggests Carol goes permanently next Monday—'I'll tell you for why—we're going in to Rickerton on Tuesday, and I thought I'd introduce her to the school and headmaster....' Mrs Marren commented that she had doubts about Mrs Tolley initially but that she seems to grow in stature.

There was a letter today from Hassex about the Hopgoods. Apparently Mrs Hopgood has been with her mother in Hassex some of the time since deserting on 15 June, but she departed on the Friday (24 June) when her mother gave her the train-fare for Marlshire. This was the weekend when we were more than half expecting her home, but she didn't come, so, unless she's returned in the meantime, we still don't know where she is.

7 July

9–10 a.m. Mr Tasker on the frustrations of working with com-mittees and for a local authority, etc.—little time to explore further frustrations.

10.15–11.30. Miss Farrar on the functions of deputy and chief caseworker. I was glad to hear her say that we needn't worry about finding foster-homes in our future areas of employment. Her idea is that you have first to settle down and know your area; this is followed by a sort of natural supply and demand. If you're doing your other work thoroughly and know a lot of people, prospective foster-parents will approach you as a result of what they've heard from friends, neighbours and relatives of foster- and adoptive-parents. In her opinion, artificial searching through advertisement and other forms of publicity bears little fruit—either attracting 'the wrong sort' (including those previously turned down) or none at all. She also divides housewives into two groups: (a) home-birds; (b) women who go out to work, or to frequent outside activities. So however strong a plea one makes for more foster-homes, while talking to the Mothers' Union or similar audiences, one is talking to the wrong group!

We've heard of extreme examples in every category during the last three days, picked out from the seniors' years of experience, including policy in some other authorities. Apparently there is one place in the north where the local rat-catcher also deals with applications for reception into care—a neo-Pied Piper as it were. In connection with the checking-up (financial and otherwise) to which fieldworkers have to submit, we heard instances of pre-psychotic workers who wrote imaginary reports on interviews when they couldn't face doing them.

Miss Gibbs attended a co-ordinating committee earlier this week, and brought back an account which is hard to believe: one case about a 'problem family' which has just been evicted. This family had lived on the estate for about ten years; stuck out like a sore thumb, and was the frequent cause of complaints from neighbours. I think there are about five children and that it's a united family. There were *no* rent arrears. The family returned from holiday recently and found their furniture on the pavement— they'd been evicted in their absence. At the co-ordinating meeting, some people voiced great concern. The housing official, whistling between his teeth, wanted no further dealings—it's somebody else's turn after ten years, though it seems other districts are being warned against rehousing the family. The housing man said he didn't care what happened to them. Somebody asked, 'Why should the children suffer?' He replied, 'It says so in the Bible—that the children are punished for the sins of the parents.'

8 July

Another letter today from Cameronshire about Mr McTavish, the woodcutter. Miss Gibbs had put him on to another department's system here of keeping tabs on any empty housing-property they see in their travels. The upshot is that he's found a cottage near his work in south Marlshire, and they move in tomorrow. He is now communicating with his relatives in Scotland and with officials—reconciliations all round—and the two older boys by the first wife are to be reunited with the Marlshire branch soon. The main question at present is whether Mr McTavish is willing to pay £10 (much reduced) for the boys' travelling expenses.

This morning I went to the county court in the south-west area with Mr Hebditch for his 'own adoption' case in which I've acted as guardian ad litem. The mother, Mr Stokes and Frances (aged 10) turned up in a taxi just as we arrived. We waited about twenty minutes together—they are quiet and simple, and seemed glad of this support. I gave Mrs Stokes the address of the MOH in her rural district, to whom she can write about her inconvenient well-water. We eventually went into a small room before Judge Blythe. The Judge spoke to Frances mainly, to see whether she understands and wanted to be adopted by Mr Stokes, and to the latter to ensure he realizes what he is doing. The Order was made, and we said goodbye outside afterwards. Frances had tears in her eyes, seeming radiant with suppressed happiness; her parents rather silent and sincere, so it was most touching. Mr Hebditch entertained me with stories of extraordinary adoptions both ways.

P.m. worked in the office.

11 July

At the University.

12 July

Can't altogether remember but quite busy. The Scottish wood-cutter has reared his head again—I'm supposed to ask him whether he will put £10 towards the older boys' fares, but we don't know his new address, except that it is on the Gradford Estate in the most southern tip of Marlshire. So it means tracing them once again. I thought for a moment I was going to have to face the Duke of Gradford, but telephoned Cameronshire instead (no help) and am going to the Gradford Estate office next week.

I went to see Mrs Victor (having heard from Gregory's mother, Mrs White) to make definite arrangements for a meeting between them all next Thursday. Mrs Victor is going to be a tower of strength in this rather fraught situation. She understands how difficult the meeting will be for the mother, who hasn't seen Gregory at all for about ten years, and we made plans accordingly.

P.m. supervision—we went over my queries about my present work. I asked Miss Farrar if she is satisfied with the way the Eamon Murphy/Mrs Almond case is going, and am glad to have received a dispensation from the Pope equal to Eamon's own. We agreed that I should go on as I am, trying to have it quiescent by the end of August; that I should see Miss Murphy once more at least, and that I should try to drive the present position well and truly home with all parties by saying, 'It's been a fair old sweat, but *worth* it, *hasn't* it?'—though I can't quite hear myself saying the latter.

In the late afternoon I went to Andersham and far beyond on two visits. First, the adoption welfare supervision (second time of asking). I haven't said much about this. It's a fairly young couple with a rather 'pretty' son Leslie (aged 10, born to them) and a 3-month-old baby, Carmen, placed for adoption. During my first visit on 17 June, Mrs Hicks protested that all was fine; that she wasn't experiencing the difficulties people had warned her to expect.... I explained my role—how it was really to support the family in what, after all, isn't an easy position. This disarmed her a little, and she asked my help over her immediate worry—i.e. filling in the adoption forms for court, over which I wasn't particularly adequate. I'm like a schoolteacher being only one chapter ahead of his class in an unaccustomed subject— but on this second visit I did seem more able to brief Mrs Hicks.

It was surprising and interesting to see a prize-card on the mantelpiece—Mrs Hicks had entered Carmen for a Baby Show last week in which she gained third place. This is perfectly natural to Mrs H, but I think I'd prefer to enter farm-stock bred by myself for a Show, rather than any human baby, especially someone else's. It certainly seems to be tempting providence during the supervision period and somehow usurps the mother's place—not that I think the incident has any great significance.

Second, a prolonged interview in a remote village to select some prospective adopters for the Marlford City voluntary adoption society. I liked Mr and Mrs Pizzy very much—country folk who keep pigs and poultry. Another link was that both Mrs P and I had done some training years ago for different things near Shrewsbury. This couple's own two children died early from cystic fibrosis. They adopted a little girl two years ago (which gave me something to go on) who is quite extraordinarily alike, physically, to Mrs Pizzy—perhaps more in mannerisms than in features, which is explicable. I won't go into all the details, but I was suddenly struck towards the end by the awful position of being partially responsible for 'giving or withholding a child' to these eager people.

13 July

Review in Rickerton Children's Home all day. Present: the home-staff, Mr Tasker, Miss Farrar, Miss Gibbs, Miss Beckwith, the educational psychologist, other fieldworkers with children there. All the children are reviewed from all aspects every six months. I'd been here long enough to find it really interesting and would have been impressed anyway.

Late afternoon: two visits in Rickerton.

First, Mrs Nash, the great-aunt of prospective Yvonne—she wasn't in, but I found her doing her job of school-caretaker, where she seems glad of visitors in between sweeping. I told her it now looks as though Yvonne might be coming to her as a foster-child from East Dowling in London. This means doing the usual vetting even though she is a relative. We've started it from an unusual angle according to East Dowling's initial request, and are now having to think (and trying to encourage East Dowling to think) of the actual people in all the ramifications of this complicated, sensational family. East Dowling asked us to interview Mrs Nash, saying that Yvonne was 'likely to present no major difficulties', but according to Yvonne's past history when earlier in care here in Marlshire, it's rapidly becoming essential for us to have recent news of Yvonne as a young adolescent and of her immediate family.

Second, I saw Mr Hopgood briefly. He still has no news of his wife. I asked whether he'd written to the last possible address I gave him last week. 'No, because she might not be there.' I'm feeling more strongly that Mrs Hopgood may procrastinate endlessly if left to return under her own steam, and that, if he wants her back, he will have to search actively and bring her back like the lost sheep. But he's got mixed feelings about her coming back, and is dependent on his more reliable relatives who hate his wife, so he concentrates on his alternating day and night shift work, and is leaving the rest to chance. He didn't sound much interested in Keith and Sam today. I said I'd bring more news of them next week.

14 July

Supervision: mostly discussing the difference between a review in a children's home and a case conference in a reception centre; the two differing functions, how they developed in Marlshire, snags and advantages of enlisting staff co-operation, selection and education and maintenance of residential staff. . . .

P.m. the big day arrived for the meeting between Mrs White, Mrs Victor and Gregory. I called for Mrs Victor at 1.45 to bring her to the office for a preliminary meeting (without Gregory) with Mrs White who was coming forty miles by train. Mrs Victor was putting a good face on her fraughtness, but said her mood had infected Gregory who already had plenty of apprehension of his own, so she was uncertain how he'd rise to the occasion. I settled Mrs Victor in the waiting room, and went outside to look out for Mrs White, who arrived promptly at 2 p.m. with her sister for moral support.

We (or rather Mrs Victor) talked for one and a quarter hours. Mrs White sat near Mrs Victor and was captivated by her in no time. Mrs Victor started by showing a recent photo of Gregory, which Mrs White studied with silent care, and then went on to describe him from the time she first fostered him at 5 years old until now, when he is 16. The whole interview was moving. Mrs Victor is sincere enough but a clever actress, and she made the whole thing live. Mrs White sat with her eyes fixed on Mrs V, laughing freely but hardly saying a word and showing nothing of her inner turmoil. There was the colour question and the illegitimacy, and the fact that mother and son hadn't met for over ten years, and Mr White doesn't know anything about it, and Mrs Victor's fear that she might lose Gregory to his white mother. Mrs V said Gregory would want to know about his father and the circumstances of his birth. She described her own role as foster-mother and how little security she has.

This afternoon was visualized as the possible beginning of a renewed relationship. Mrs Victor had three requests to make of Mrs White:

(a) Be *kind* to Gregory.

(b) Be *gentle* with him (poor Mrs White sat looking the epitome of harmlessness).

(c) Don't give him too many presents, if any. Mrs Victor realized that Mrs White might well give presents in attempted reparation, but said it would upset Gregory and her other foster-children.

Mrs Victor finally told Mrs White what Gregory already knows about his mother; she said she'd always told him that his mother had done her utmost to support him, and had only parted with him when it became impossible to carry on. At this point, Mrs White broke down completely for a few moments, and I think we were vaguely relieved. We had another cigarette all round and talked generally while Mrs White recomposed herself externally. Then I drove them to the foster-home and had to leave them to it, not being invited. In a way I should have liked to be present. I shall see Mrs Victor next week, and told Mrs White that I'm available until the end of August.

15 July

A.m. finishing reports etc. A long afternoon at Redlands case conference. Since Keith and Sam Hopgood went there, I'd done social histories, and Miss Grainger (educational psychologist) had tested them. I saw her reports today—they fitted amazingly. Both results were unrealistic about IQ, as Sam has unusually small powers of concentration and Keith, she said, was one of the most difficult children she'd tested. She's exceptionally easy in manner, but couldn't reach Keith at all for some time, 'and under no circumstances would he draw me a man'.

About a dozen cases were discussed with senior officers, relevant fieldworkers, students, residential staff and other representatives of interested agencies. Carol (with 'my' Tolleys) came first. Mrs Marren described her settling in her new foster-home extremely well in every way—which is believable because of her interim displays of temperament. (We'd talked earlier in the office about the change in a child after leaving a children's home for a foster-home—Mrs Marren could only convey that Carol now looks 'lighter'—i.e. in terms of inward levitation rather than avoirdupois.)

Then it emerged during the conference that some of Mrs Willcox's jewellery was discovered under Carol's mattress after she left, and more ear-rings are missing, so Carol is suspected. It was decided that Carol must be told about this but Mrs Marren was going on leave immediately, so I am to do it. Mrs Marren and I had a brief word outside the room about how best to do it, and then I went back to introduce discussion on the new children, Keith and Sam. It took a longish time to present the family circumstances. Then Miss Grainger made her report, and the residential staff spoke of mutual affection beginning to grow in spite of the problems. Then decisions were made with a speed which left me reeling:

(a) The children's future must be settled very soon.

(b) I am to explain to Mr Hopgood, and discuss it and, *if* his wife is coming back, he and I have to find her within three weeks.

(c) Otherwise (or perhaps even if she returns) a Section 2 resolution will be made, assuming parental rights in respect of Mrs H, but not of Mr Hopgood.

(d) I'm to make a report for (c) with regard to Mrs H's 'habits and mode of life'.

(e) Mr Hopgood must by hook or by crook see his children.

(f) Keith and Sam mustn't stay at Redlands long enough to form real attachments. If Marlshire assumes parental rights under Section 2, they are to move to Downbanks Children's Home within a month.

(The above and Carol means quite a lot extra to do and I'm already booked up for next week, what with appointments already made, and having to be 'office girl' for three days. This is one of the features of field social work—trying to fit in essentials.)

It was nice to meet the three Collingham students again. After tea, I made an inventory of her wretched missing jewellery with Mrs Willcox who is a very motherly person with a big enough bosom not to require much extra ornamentation in my private opinion. The children look forward to these special days and meeting their own social workers. It's not easy to talk with Keith and Sam—I'll have to send postcards in between instead. Keith vanished at my mention of his father.

16 July (Saturday morning)

This was the duty morning previously fixed for this weekend—surprisingly peaceful, so got on with reports and letters. I received a very nice letter from Mrs White, Gregory's mother—thanking me for 'making it so easy' for her to meet Gregory and for standing by, and saying that Gregory has 'grown a Lovely

83

Boy', and it was an enjoyable afternoon and he'd walked with her to the station to see her off. Miss Farrar wants me to see her again, and get her to 'face' telling her husband about Gregory.

We also discussed my coming interview with Carol about the jewellery. Mrs Marren (having had little time for thought before going on leave) wanted me to do it in such a way that Mrs Tolley shouldn't know. In a way I'm doing this for Mrs Marren, and it's unfortunate for her that I'm Miss Farrar's student, because of course we must 'face' telling the foster-mother. And I do think this best myself in the circumstances, for the sake of expediency as well.

This morning I wrote letters with a view to cutting down interviewing time next week—i.e. introducing the subject needing discussion in advance, to give people time to think beforehand—I haven't tried this before but it seems sensible if there's only a short time-limit before something must be settled. There are a tremendous number of plain facts to be remembered—it's a bit irritating to think I shall have to drop them and start imbibing new ones in the space of a weekend when starting work in Loamshire at the end of August.

18 July

A.m. worked in the office. I went to Mrs Burke (senior administrator) to be briefed for doing the job of office girl for three days of the real one's holiday. Working the switch-board sounded the most alarming aspect so I went to Mr Parfit for a few minutes' preliminary instruction—I think he made it extra complicated on purpose because I couldn't see myself managing the thing at all. I also took a quick look at the tea-making arrangements. I was almost pleased to find that the sixteen-odd people mostly have their own cup/mug which you have to remember, because the department seems too efficient for that sort of thing at first. Fortunately most of the cups have something in common with their owners, being straight up and down, or bulbous, or a tiny bit cracked, etc. One typist who takes herself very seriously has a beaker inscribed: To thine own self be true. Anyway I don't start this till Wednesday.

I composed official letters to other authorities in an effort to trace Mrs Hopgood, and to East Dowling about Yvonne and Mrs Nash. I phoned Mrs Tolley, and arranged to meet Carol out of school tomorrow to ask her about this jewellery she's supposed to have taken. I told Mrs Tolley about it and she took it very well. I asked her not to say anything about it to worry Carol meanwhile, and said I wished I knew Carol better. Mrs Tolley gave me a tip: that she finds Carol reacts more successfully to a 'straight-from-the-shoulder than a smooth approach'.

A message came this morning to say there is a vacancy at last for Jimmy Best in Drayton Special Class. This was planned before I started here, and now I learnt that his foster-mother, Mrs Yates (a very simple old soul with a stammer except, I'm told, 'when she tries to pull a fast one'), would have to be persuaded to agree to Jimmy's having special education—she'd tend to regard such a suggestion as a slight to herself or the foster-child. So I thought I'd better see her straightaway and went this lunchtime. It seemed partly to be a matter of using guile or power—it's not easy to see where to draw the line, especially in a statutory service. It turned out that Mrs Yates did agree, because of three factors:

(a) When I began to explain, she got the wrong end of the stick and thought Jimmy was having to go away to boarding school. She was so relieved that it simply means a change in the same town by day that she was disarmed. Someone reading my report afterwards thought I'd done this deliberately, and thought it rather bright—but I would think it taking guile too far.

(b) I said that special help now, particularly with reading, should enable Jimmy to take his place in ordinary secondary schooling later. This is the official view, and Mrs Yates wants Jimmy to reach as high a status as her older foster-child, George.

(c) My main line, which was most effective. I know from listening to Mrs Yates earlier that it means a tremendous amount to her that she managed to rear Jimmy after he came to her 'in a pitiful state of iglect' at 2 years old. So I mentioned this again, and continued by saying that she herself had largely overcome this early stage, as Jimmy at 10 years old seems really healthy and happy but the early neglect means he is still a bit backward at school, and she would be helping him further by approving of the special class idea. This appealed to her very much. I suppose it's possible to use this sort of strategy if it's true, and likely to produce a desirable effect.

2.00 p.m. East Marlshire Area case sub-committee at Brayley Children's Home—my last one—they don't meet in August. It's held here once a quarter with a preliminary meeting about the Home itself. The committee seems a fraction less formal in this setting. I reported the Hopgood children again.

19 July

A full day. After a bit of office work, I set off at about 9.15 on another woodcutter hunt to the farthest tip of Marlshire in low cloud and heavy rain. First I called at the south area office, just to explain briefly about the McTavish family now living in their area, and to ask where the Gradford Estate office is, and for any tips in enlisting its assistance.

I went to the Gradford place, to ask if Mr McTavish has one of their cottages and if so, where. He hasn't, but the agent recalled referring Mr McT to Lord Dogwood's agent on the adjoining estate. He got the Dogwood agent on the phone for me, and I found that the McTavishes have a cottage at Jacob's Ladder, which seems to be off the map. It took nearly the rest of the morning to find this—a row of six uninhabited-looking cottages, not near anywhere. The woodcutter's cottage has a wealth of weeds growing through its doorstep, and is much the same inside.

As usual at the end of these tracing expeditions, I'm almost amazed actually to find the person I was looking for, and can hardly believe they've remained ignorant of my difficult approach—you'd think their ears would be burning at least, though it's worth realizing that a 'missing person' (such as Mrs Hopgood) doesn't ever regard herself as such, knowing perfectly well herself where she is all the time and being hardly aware that others don't know. This is the second time I've met Mrs McTavish, and today we had quite a laugh together that I'd had to find her a second time—it easily mightn't have seemed funny to either of us. Last time she was stolidly sullen.

The change seems to date from Miss Gibbs's interview with Mr McT, and the fact that this family now has a clearer conscience, having been helped by Cameronshire and Marlshire departments towards reuniting themselves. The good work was certainly begun by us but has reached a stage where the family branches in Marlshire and Scotland are in closer touch than we, whose right hand hardly knows what our left hand is doing, and so we have to ask the family itself—which is healthy enough even if it makes us look a little ridiculous. I heard the plans for the two older sons of the first marriage coming in early August, and asked if they can raise £10 for travelling expenses. Mrs McTavish showed me round the cottage, and the efforts they're making towards re-decorating and preparing for the coming boys. It's an odd place, like a town slum in the depths of the country. The sight of weeds getting the better of solid stone can be heartening or depressing—the latter in this case I think. I may meet this family again when it's complete.

I hurried back to Marlford, got back at 2 p.m. At 2.15 p.m. Miss Gibbs and I went to a co-ordinating meeting which I particularly wanted to attend because my first short-stay family was on the agenda: Mrs Chubb of Crossbridge, with Linda, Susan, Tracey and the newish baby, Jayne. There was no housing representative present, but they seem to be pressing a policy of eviction just now. Mrs Chubb is almost certain to be evicted. Various parties agreed that she's deteriorated greatly since she started to cohabit with the 18-year-old mentally handi-capped boy, Gary (though it could be more a matter of accumu-lating children), and there seem to be two or three more men there now. Those of us who know it at first hand agreed there is much positive about the family.

The chairman thought eviction would give Mrs Chubb 'the necessary jolt to make her pull her socks up', but I don't think someone like Mrs Chubb can be jolted into conformity—it's more likely to turn her sour and apathetic. Another representative thought she should be 'made to choose' between Gary and her children. We think she'd choose the children, but I know she's really fond of Gary whatever we think of him, and it seems hard to blackmail her affections by threatening the loss of her home, when she'd be independent if she had more money and intelli-gence. There do seem to be some very strict officials in this part of the world, though perhaps they lurk under stones everywhere and are especially liable to crawl out where other people's children are involved.

I had to crawl out myself before the above meeting ended, in order to go and meet Carol out of school at 4 p.m. I'd rather dreaded this, but was too busy today to incubate apprehension, which is one advantage of a caseload with plenty of different eggs in one's basket. I'd only met Carol in the past when she was often sulky and ignored me. For her, she was quite friendly today. I began tackling her straightaway in order to get through what I was supposed to do. I have a slight horror of prolonged questioning about wrong-doing after my previous job at Downcroft, but this was from different motives, only it's awkward when you are never likely to know the 'real truth'. And Carol is committed to care for larceny and for being beyond her mother's control; also she has attended child guidance for several years. I could have been relatively cosy with her about stealing in a child guidance setting, but not here to the same extent.

Carol listened while I told her about our meeting at Redlands last week, how we'd heard about the jewellery being found under her mattress after she left, and the ear-rings still missing and the evidence pointing to her, and how we hoped she might be able to throw light, and how Mrs Marren would like to have seen her now but is on leave, and that Mrs Tolley knows about it but not her mother. Carol denied the whole thing but was unexpectedly co-operative. I'd thought she'd withdraw into sulks or tears, and had feared it might jeopardize the early fostering situation. Her attitude was rather convincing, and she mentioned one domestic detail in her defence which seemed most unlikely but which turned out to be true when I was asked to check with the Redlands staff afterwards. Anyway, it's clear enough to me that, if Carol took the trouble initially to steal jewellery, it'd be illogical for her to leave Redlands forgetting it under her mattress, unless she perhaps perversely hoped to be brought back to Redlands as a 'punishment' for theft.

So I really got nowhere except in doing as I'd been asked. I finished by saying that if she hadn't taken the things there is no need to worry but, if she had, she might slowly decide it best to get it off her chest to somebody—perhaps to Mrs Marren later. Mrs Tolley met us pleasantly on the door-step, trying to read our faces. Carol went to change into play-clothes, and Mrs Tolley asked me how we'd got on. I told her briefly. She replied that she didn't want 'to shelter Carol', but wonders whether another child could have put the jewellery under Carol's vacated mattress—which is what I think. We agreed that Mrs Tolley won't pursue it, unless Carol confides in her. I thought Mrs T reacted very well. She seems more contented since Carol went there— there's no longer the feeling that you'll never get away from the Ancient Mariner telling an endless tale.

She and Carol and I had a cup of tea together and talked generally. They seem to be fitting happily—all of them, in which case Carol no longer needs to leave caches of jewellery in order to engineer her own removal, and it's best forgotten. Things do seem to work together in this family—for example, Carol leaves the farm at 8.20 a.m. with the milk van which coincides with the school bus at 8.30, so her journey isn't made more difficult by living in an isolated farm. Carol enjoyed showing me her new clothes, and asked me to post a letter to her mother when I left. I said a final goodbye to them all, not expecting to see them again.

Miss Farrar was fairly satisfied, but wanted me to make another similar attempt next week—she thinks I'm 'in a better position to clear it up properly' than Mrs Marren. I don't want to

(a) Because I don't like it. It's not so bad once, but I don't like it dragging on any more than Carol would.

(b) I don't see that I can clear it any further. I gathered the main aim was for Carol to know that we knew; to give her a chance to speak, and to make some investment against possible future theft. I did that, and it's stuck at this point unless Carol chooses to volunteer more spontaneously. It might be easier for her to tell Mrs Marren, whom she knows and likes and who didn't have to start this off, but harder if I keep pumping in between.

(c) There was an implicit understanding between us all at the time that it was happening once. A second campaign wouldn't ring true: it would start at a disadvantage and put an unnecessary strain on the foster-home, especially when I've said goodbye.

(d) In short, one can only do this sort of thing once. It may be bad for a girl like Carol to think she's got away with stealing; it's just as bad to force her to continue lying about having stolen. It's equally bad to accuse her of something she hasn't done. Even Carol mayn't be sure whether she has stolen—we certainly aren't and probably never shall be. So I think that unless you are sure, it's reasonable to ask only once. It may be different if you have what's known as 'a good relationship' with the person concerned because that would carry you both on naturally.

Anyway, when I'd argued slightly on the above lines, it seems Miss Farrar isn't going to be quite so stickling, and I may only have to ring Mrs Tolley about it next week, and then Mrs Marren will be back and I shall have to tell her that I didn't do it on the lines she herself suggested. This extreme business of being forced, and forcing others, to face things is giving me amusement, nasty moments, more confidence, and is quite therapeutic taken all round! If I make an index at the back of this diary, there will be a lot listed under 'Face'.

Lastly I went to see Mr Hopgood, and enlarged on my letter by explaining a little what has been decided at Redlands about Keith and Sam, and how we want to make a special effort to find his wife because she's in danger of losing her parental rights. I told him I'd written some letters, and hope he'll join in. He seems a fraction more positive about wanting her back; he agreed she probably cares more about her children than is apparent. I also said we think it important for him to visit the boys, and he's going to try. Part of his reluctance to visit is that he fears Sam will cry when he leaves again (and possibly the poor reception he's likely to have from Keith) so we discussed this and he seemed more able to consider visiting them.

20 July

I started three days as 'office girl'—the first task is to unlock the post-box and bring up the letters for a little ceremony. I slit the envelopes, Mr Parfit extracts the papers and stamps them with a grid plus date, Mrs Burke glances through and initials them for passage. Meanwhile I check the empty envelopes, and collect material from the out-trays in other rooms. Then deliver the post. And all the time the switch-board keeps buzzing. The first call I tried to take turned out to be for me, so I was surprised and relieved not to have to put it through. It was a Rickerton health visitor to say she's heard from Mrs Hopgood saying she very much wants to come home and 'to turn over a new leaf'. I've kept in touch with this HV from the beginning, and now she preferred me to reply to Mrs Hopgood. I did—telling her where her children are, asking her to write direct to her husband, saying I'm sure he wants her back, and that I look forward to meeting her.

10 a.m. making tea and taking it round on a noisy trolley, keeping to a routine path. I'd found the administrative staff reasonably friendly before, but quite different when it comes to my doing office work which is inferior to theirs, and especially

when giving them cups of tea. One even said jokingly that this was 'good for human relations'. I gained quite a new angle on the whole department during the three days, besides learning something about office work (which is more complex than I realized), plus being able to link up some bits of procedure which weren't clear when working only in the team's room. The switch-board wasn't too bad—quite possible when not going at full strength.

In between whiles Mr Parfit and I got on with filing—a sort of fairy-tale punishment because it was a fortnight behind with his being on holiday recently. The papers are covered with official squiggles by this stage which all mean something. After the p.m. tea-round you start on the out-going post—folding, sealing, weighing, stamping, booking letters and parcels. At the end of the day, Mr Parfit hoped I hadn't 'overworked' and I couldn't make out whether he was teasing.

21 July

The same, except that the three Collingham students and I went to an imposing County Council meeting at 11 a.m.—there were some lively exchanges and we enjoyed having lunch together afterwards.

22 July

The same, only more so. In an excess of zeal I rechecked that the empty letter-box really was empty, and found a personal letter for me. Also I heard from Mr Hopgood, writing to say he'd heard from his wife too, and has replied saying he wants her back. I rang Mrs Willcox at Redlands about Keith and Sam, and Carol. There is a general mixed feeling about Mrs Hopgood coming home, but that we'll have to make the best of it—we plan to return her children to her gradually, and continue visiting her afterwards.

Supervision session in the morning, otherwise a full last day as office girl and did some stencilling. People were in quite a glow when I distributed their final cups of tea—I wonder if it'll be any different next week. I see the ranks of the administrative staff more clearly having worked from the very bottom—previously I didn't know the difference between a pool typist and a clerk. Some of them expect to be waited on and some don't, and you can read quite a lot about their status from the characters of their tea-cups—before it reaches the tea-leaf stage. Mr Tasker is the only one with a saucer, which I daresay is the office staff's own idea of what's due to him.

25 July

Another letter from Mr Hopgood, 'Just a line to say my wife has returned. . . .' I wrote to Eamon's mother, Miss Murphy, to ask whether we may meet again 'to discuss Eamon's progress'.

There is yet another letter from Cameronshire about the McTavishes. Our right hand isn't synchronizing with the left at all now—it sounds as though the children are there already, and the paternal grandmother in Scotland is 'so ambivalent' that she may pick a quarrel in order to have an excuse to take the children back to Cameron, so will I visit again quickly. Miss Farrar says I can reply saying it's too far for me to go again this week. I gather some Scottish departments board-out their children in the wilds with crofters, where life is so simple that there's not much scope for things to gang agley. Life seems equally primitive down here at Jacob's Ladder. I wrote to my branch of the wood-cutter family, asking them in effect to tell me what's happening straight from the horse's mouth.

Sequel to the co-ordinating committee's discussion about the Chubb family: it was decided that NSPCC should be responsible. Financial assistance has ceased because Mrs Chubb is cohabiting—this is why she is told she must choose between her 18-year-old man, Gary, and her four children. The NSPCC Inspector, Mr Worth, visited her the day after the meeting and gave her 'seven days to pull herself together'. On Friday he found that Gary had 'bought a car out of his pocket money'. At 2.30 a.m. that night they all flitted in the car, driven by Gary, with four children aged under 6. They obviously cannot live for long in a car, and I'm very sorry about it. We expect the police to pick them up any day.

Miss Farrar and I spent most of today at Loamshire County Hall with our opposite numbers (i.e. their deputy supervising a fellow-student of mine)—it's good of her to arrange this so that I can compare administration and policy in the two counties. Loamshire seems more relaxed though very much up and coming, whereas Marlshire may be at its peak of efficiency, assuming some educative role towards other authorities. We started at Miss Farrar's instigation with my 'rights and duties' as a future employee in Loamshire, and then I startled their deputy so much with the first item on my list of administrative questions (which Miss F had asked me to prepare beforehand) that I hadn't the nerve to continue, but it set a comprehensive ball rolling which was interesting, amusing and a fraction bewildering, and we continued in the afternoon, after a pleasant lunch in the deputy's home—she is far more concerned to feed students than to plump them up with knowledge. Miss Farrar asked whether I could have a list of my future caseload before starting in south Loamshire— I said I'd like to have the Chubb family if they should happen to turn up.

26 July

I'm just beginning to have the feel of a proper caseload (even though my present one is nowhere near full numbers) or at least to appreciate the economics of greater numbers. Previously I seem to have been all over the place, but am reaching the stage where I can make more than one visit in the same town, or telephone another agency about more than one situation, and then duplicate the conversation on memo forms (am on my third pad of memo forms and would be fairly interested in a freak green one now).

I went to see the West Indian foster-mother, Mrs Victor, this morning, wanting to hear about the meeting between Gregory and his mother Mrs White, and Gregory's reactions—also to begin arranging the same thing for Joe. (We have just heard via the education welfare officer that Joe's mother, Mrs Kemp, previously unwilling to have anything to do with Joe, is now slightly willing.)

All this has been more painful to Mrs Victor than she realizes, I think, though she does enjoy recounting it and acting the various parts. It had been an unexpectedly happy afternoon on 14 July, with the general verdict that a delicate situation had been managed as easily as possible. Joe had stuck to Gregory's side 'like a blood brother', and they'd spent time alone with Mrs White while she told Gregory something about herself and his background. Gregory is a thinker. A few days later he asked Mrs Victor, 'What did you think of her then?'

'Oh—well, I thought she was a nice little thing. . . .'

'Is that *all*?'

'Well—I thought she was quite nice. . . .'

'Only *quite*?'

'I thought she was very nice—she's clean and kind-hearted, but not very educated—she hasn't had your advantages—'

'Oh.'

Mrs Victor realizes in theory that Gregory needs to assess his parents in relation to himself. Later, after more thought, he said that he'd wanted to meet his mother, and was very glad he has, but is now satisfied to leave it there. He can't easily think of her as his mother, and touched Mrs Victor by adding that he continues to feel she is his real mother. Mrs V surprised me by saying that she hadn't heard from Mrs White, who I know intended to write. So I repeated what Mrs White had written to me about her gratitude to Mrs Victor and that she thought her 'wonderful', and also expressed my own appreciation over the way Mrs Victor coped with the meeting.

She went on to mention casually that Joe had said he'd like to see his mother now. I was pleased to have this opening for the next stage, but Mrs Victor continued that she'd told Joe he mustn't ask for this glibly—if he has 'a deep and sincere desire, say in six months or a year', she will see about it. I explained about Miss Farrar being responsible for the boys (though Marlford City supervises them here); how I'm a student in the county department until the end of August; that Miss Farrar had asked me to arrange a meeting between both boys and their mothers, and why she thinks it important, and that I'm hoping to meet Joe's mother, Mrs Kemp, next week.

Mrs Victor told me she was never afraid for Gregory to meet his mother (though she was naturally apprehensive at the time) but she is afraid of Joe meeting his. She told me the little she knows of Mrs Kemp, which we compared with the little I know. Mrs Victor builds up a picture of what she imagines her foster-children's parents are like, also she says she has 'an intuitive feeling' about someone she is due to meet, and she has adverse feelings about Mrs Kemp, being almost sure she'll be 'blowsy' and. . . . I supplied the word 'coarse', at which Mrs Victor clutched.

There was nothing she could take exception to (or really get hold of) in Gregory's rather colourless mother, but she feels strongly that Mrs Kemp won't be a person to whom Joe could aspire in any way—'because there's a "coarse" streak in Joe'. He's an easily influenced, happy-go-lucky person, she said (on probation for a year earlier) who needs very firm handling. Mrs Victor described the consistent efforts she's made over many years to root out Joe's less pleasant traits. He's nearly 13 now. She is terrified that, if he meets his mother, he will make what he finds an excuse for going downhill. Other stumbling blocks Mrs Victor produced include:

(a) She fears Mrs Kemp may want Joe 'home' now he's nearly wage-earning. She doesn't quite see how unlikely it is for these married white mothers in pure white rural areas to want their half-caste sons home. She said with awe at one point, 'And you know, Joe is beautiful'—he is, above all to Mrs Victor who has cared for him all these years.

(b) She is a 'great believer in timing', as I am, and thinks we must wait for a time when things will have moved together for a meeting to seem fitting.

(c) She would want to meet Mrs Kemp herself first (like Mrs White) but she would want longer in between to feel ready for Mrs Kemp and Joe to meet. She could only go with me for such a meeting next week, which is really too soon for me and Mrs Kemp. And we'd have to take her younger foster-children with us—'and watch our conversation because they have long ears'.

(d) Joe is away at camp for two weeks in August. Mrs Victor has booked trips for virtually the whole month and will be out daily!

We must obviously take Mrs Victor's ideas and feelings very seriously. I think there is even more to it. She'd say herself that she loves all her foster-children alike, but it seemed apparent to me today that she has a special love for Joe. I said I see it is asking a lot of her to want to introduce two mothers in such a short space of time, but she won't altogether admit to this. She has a very strong personality, and puts all of herself into her fosterings for the sake of each whole child. She has enjoyed a measure of autonomy from the very nature of these foster-children, and naturally enough feels possessive towards them. I am always mindful of the fact that this is a Marlford City foster-home, with their fieldworker supervising Miss Farrar's children there; that Mrs Victor is vital to Marlford City and such a capable person that she's had a pretty free hand all these years.

I'm also mindful of the fact that Miss Farrar wants this job done! I'd like to do it, but it begins to look impossible from the time aspect alone. So it's a delicate situation within a delicate situation, and I don't seem to go very long without one. I wonder sometimes whether they'd be quite so delicate if I weren't involved in them, but can't really know, any more than I can know I'd live ten years longer (as someone once suggested) if I'd stayed in farming rather than moving to social work.

I left it with Mrs Victor that I'm responsible to Miss Farrar (I might as well take any advantage of my lowly position); that I will discuss all this fully with Miss Farrar before trying to go any further, because I see the force of Mrs Victor's feelings and the rightness of them; but that we could at least meet Mrs Kemp before deciding she's coarse and an undesirable influence. There's also Mrs Kemp to consider—she may just be steeling herself to meet Joe, and won't easily understand that more unwillingness comes from Joe's side. If we do arrange a meeting between them before I leave, it will be a case of driving several horses to the water with them reluctant to drink.

(I had another letter from Gregory's mother next day. She is very sorry I'm leaving and wants to meet me again before I go. I seem to have made a hit with her, though it's like talking to a white ghost when I'm actually with her.)

In the afternoon I went to see people in Rickerton. I went first to Mrs Chapel—the 'private' foster-home where Keith and Sam proved too much within twenty-four hours, to see if it seemed to need salvaging for Miss Beckwith's future use, and to make some attempt to do this. Mrs Chapel was quite pleased to see me (still sublimely unaware that it was drastic for her to reject foster-children so quickly even if they were abnormally difficult to handle)—she would have liked a Hopgood gossip, but I think is secure for any future 'good' foster-children that may turn up. She returned Keith's raincoat which we'd forgotten when I moved them to Redlands.

Then I went to meet Mrs Hopgood! Mr Hopgood opened the door, and I entered their own home for the first time. He told me that she came home last Friday; they collected the baby, Karen, from his sister's on Saturday, and now Mrs Hopgood was distempering the bedrooms (reminiscent of a returned approved school absconder) as an important external gesture, I gathered, towards having things nice for Keith and Sam to come home again.

Mrs Hopgood came downstairs, after I'd asked to meet her, and shook hands very hesitantly. She looks young, ill and tired, with the bit of refinement that often seems to be produced at Hawthorn Grange—the particular approved school where she was in her teens. I can see a lot of Keith and Sam in her face, especially their vulnerability. I am supposed to rub things well in now, and not make it too easy for her to have her children home. In fact I think her spirit is thoroughly willing—it's the flesh that needs support over a long period of time.

She was constrained, nervous and near tears throughout this first joint interview, but seems to have reached some understanding with Mr H, who looks (for him) a fraction more spruce, with brighter eyes. I started by asking what she hoped to do about Keith and Sam. 'Have them home as soon as possible.' I explained how we'd been about to plan their long-term care, and described a bit the effect on both boys. She listened miserably about Keith, but had to smile when I spoke of Sam. I suggested we should go together to see the boys on Thursday, and work towards bringing them home the following week. She agreed gladly. Mr Hopgood is still on night shifts but asked if he and Karen could come too. They received Keith's raincoat as a token of more to follow.

27 July

I wrote to the other counties from which I'd sought help in finding Mrs Hopgood, saying she's home. We've had a report from Hassex and are beginning to piece together Mrs Hopgood's doings whilst away. She went off with a married Rickerton man, then turned up alone at her mother's in Hassex; during the weekend of 24–27 June (when we half-expected her back and the boys came into care) she went to her newly-married sister's in London. After a few days, her sister went into hospital for her confinement, and the sister's husband and Mrs Hopgood lived together until she wrote to say she wanted to come home. I telephoned Redlands, where the staff have mixed feelings now, arranging to visit with the Hopgood parents tomorrow.

In the afternoon I went to Drayton to see Mrs Almond and Eamon. As I rounded the last corner, I saw a little group of people making off rapidly in the rain. I recognized Mrs Almond in the rear, and she came over to speak to me—very flustered. She was just off on an outing with Eamon, Miss Murphy and a fourth person—perhaps Miss M's married sister about whom feelings also run deep. They looked awkward and I could see my presence was an embarrassment. Eamon at least seemed perfectly at ease; he left his mother's side and came over to say hello. I smiled across some distance to Miss Murphy, but couldn't make out if she was smiling back or grimacing against the rain-drops, and felt it was hardly opportune to tackle her about my having written to suggest another meeting.

(Miss Murphy hasn't replied and probably doesn't want to meet me, which doesn't quite fit with Miss Farrar's idea that I have control over these separate parties and have brought them all to heel.) Meanwhile, Mrs Almond was too confused to know what she was saying—she'd be glad to see me any *other* time or to 'contact you personally'—so I said goodbye and drove on. In a way it's heartening to see them going off together like that, but would have been more so if I could have met them all easily. It's sufficient for me if they're happier among themselves, and I may have interfered too much already.

Then I had an extraordinary time in Pilbury: a new case, which might be much or little. It started with a recent letter from the German welfare authority asking for a visit to be paid to a family which has just come to England to see how they're settling: to see how Erika is, and to give the mother advice in handling this daughter. On arrival, I found Mrs Strickland is German; she has a 10-year-old illegitimate daughter, Erika, who spent her first two years in a nursery in Germany, and the next four years with her maternal grandparents, where the grandfather drank (Mrs Strickland told me) causing much unpleasantness, the grandmother couldn't control Erika, and there was 'a mental sick woman' also in the house whose 'young son knocked about'. During the last four years Mrs Strickland has been living with a British soldier. They have a $3\frac{1}{2}$-year-old daughter, Rosa, who is to be registered as British and legitimate.

Mrs Strickland largely took over the care of Erika since her association with Mr Strickland. The family came over in April; they married here and their baby son, Richard, was born in May. I arrived on a miserably wet afternoon without an appointment.

Mr and Mrs Strickland, Rosa and Richard were in the living room. Erika, I heard, was in her bedroom upstairs. Mrs Strickland speaks English well. The most striking thing about her is a scar running down her left cheek; both she and her husband show more character than good looks in their faces. Mrs Strickland began to tell me the above, and of her difficulties with Erika.

Mr Strickland didn't speak at all for a long time. He was nursing the baby, and completely engrossed in watching its every move; he had a tender expression and looked much gentler than his wife. I was startled when he interrupted his wife with extreme roughness, saying, 'You might as well tell her the truth about Erika.' I found that this is the tone he reserves to speak of Erika— he dotes on his own two children, who seem content with both parents, though well-disciplined.

Mrs Strickland gave me a long string of complaints about Erika: always been difficult, always temper-tantrums so that her mother is now almost physically afraid of her at 10 years old and dreads the future, always *wanting* more and never satisfied although Mrs S protested that she receives a generous (material) share, won't help in the house except at the pistol's point, bullies her mother with 'bad words' but is afraid of Mr Strickland (repeating the pattern with her grandparents), runs out of the house at night when she's expected to go to bed at 7.30 (Rosa's bedtime), wets her pants constantly although German and English doctors have said there's no need for it, urinates on her bedroom floor, bites her nails, and her school report says her behaviour 'wants watching, so that proves Erika isn't only difficult at home'—plus a further indefinable something which Mrs Strickland could only convey by clenching her fists and gritting her teeth.

A year ago Erika stole three bicycles and was subsequently in a home for difficult children in Germany. This was a great shock to her mother, who in all her years of work has never taken so much as a pin. When the family was coming to England, it was hard to decide what to do with Erika; Mrs S thought her own parents unsuitable to have charge of a child. Mr Strickland has known Erika for four years, and has no use or tolerance for her. Mrs S swore she wouldn't marry him unless Erika could come too. Now she is landed with Erika in a foreign country, plus her own guilty, ambivalent feelings (negative side uppermost now) and is at her wit's end—but (a constant refrain) she will not risk her marriage with Mr Strickland.

We discussed this for some time and I suggested the possibility of child guidance if the clinic here could take them on. I explained the set-up, and found that Mrs S had tried something similar in Germany for what sounded like two diagnostic interviews. She'd be willing to try, realizing it would mean both herself and Erika attending for some time. This was really as much as I could do today—to have their impressions and begin to suggest some action. I asked if I could just meet Erika before going, but that there was no need for her to think I'd come specially about her. Perhaps Mrs S misunderstood. She told Rosa (who is sharply required to 'Speak English!' on the rare occasions when she reverts to her native tongue) to tell Erika to come downstairs. Rosa did so, and then barred the door into the room so that it took several seconds of gentle pushing before Erika could gain entry. The Stricklands ignored this.

Erika went straight to her mother's side, who said without looking up, 'This lady wants to speak to you.' Erika came quickly and stood very close just behind my chair, looking ahead with a set face and standing rigidly almost to attention. I've never experienced anything like this in a private house, or not quite, and felt a bit shattered. The whole atmosphere is one of explosive violence, barely below the surface. I could only ask her a few gentle questions such as whether she prefers her name spelt with a k or a c, if she likes England and school, and about her chief interest of swimming. She answered as though I was bullying, so I gave up. The awful thing was that she continued standing there, quite immobile with defiant submission, waiting.

I tried to draw her into a table game between Rosa and her father which was going on under our noses—Erika seemed half-willing, but the others weren't, only it broke the immediate deadlock. The others don't seem to speak directly to her—they just use this brutal tone in speaking of her. Erika looks healthy physically—stocky, with short brown hair and foreign curves to her nose and mouth. It is the expression on her face which is what Miss Farrar would call 'Terrible, really'. It's reminiscent of the wild, stony look Beethoven had after his deafness cut him off to some extent from music and people, or the expression I imagine the Spartan boy wore when the fox was biting. (I forgot to say there is 'no reason' for Erika to be jealous of Rosa, but the two have to be kept separate which means that Erika is often alone in her bedroom.)

Mrs Strickland probably expected me to give Erika a good telling off there and then; when she saw this wasn't forthcoming, she proceeded to re-list her complaints against Erika, concluding: 'All I want is for Erika to treat me like her mother and not like dirt . . . but I will not risk my marriage. . . .' This was awkward with Erika present, but I cut it as short as possible and said goodbye. Erika just managed to smile back at me. I had another word with Mrs Strickland on the door-step, as she seemed reluctant to let me go—I told her I'll try to arrange help and will be in touch. She and her husband are in a dilemma, I can see, but it's unthinkable what Erika must be suffering, in a strange country too.

I wrote a full report, with a view to child guidance which I hope will agree to try. It's obviously beyond the advice-giving stage, and would be difficult for the same person to work with both mother and daughter. But whether the situation will survive long enough to ease with child guidance techniques, I almost doubt. The alternative is for Erika to be received into care, but it would need to be special care, and perhaps would require committal. The weather made it worse somehow—it has a nightmare quality, looking back.

28 July

First a little work in the office. At 10 a.m. I called for the Hopgoods in Rickerton. Mrs H was ready to come to Redlands with Karen, but Mr H was still asleep, having worked an extra long shift. Anyway I was glad he'd thought of coming at all, and to have more opportunity to talk with Mrs Hopgood by herself. She said a lot during our hundred mile journey there and back.

She started by saying she thought she'd seen me before. I reminded her of her previous worker, and said I might conceivably have seen her when she was at Hawthorn Grange. She'd almost forgotten having been at an approved school, but said it was the first place where she'd known any happiness, and that she can't remember things, as her mind is clouded over nowadays. She talked a bit about Hawthorn Grange, and about her Hassex childhood, which she feels was a hard one. She is very disappointed that her mother 'no longer seems interested' in her, but seems to have transferred her earlier hopes (of her mother coming to the rescue) to equally unrealistic wishes of winning enough money to buy a luxury caravan and live in the heart of a wood with her husband and children, away from their unsympathetic neighbours and her in-laws in Rickerton.

She said, 'I don't know if you can understand, but everything had got so tight inside that I really had to run away....' (It's really very like an approved school absconding.) She wanted sympathy about her health and tiredness, telling me she hadn't had a good night's sleep during her desertion with worrying about the children. We talked about them more. She admits she is fonder of Sam; that Keith's 'sly defiance' infuriates her as well as the way her in-laws favour him as though he were the odd-man-out. She asked fairly early on if she could possibly have the boys back today, adding humbly that she's nearly finished the distempering. I'd have liked to say yes immediately, but was supposed to plan a gradual return, so said we'd see how the first meeting went and what seemed best. . . .

We arrived at Redlands just before lunch and saw Mrs Willcox. We went to the window to call Keith, who was playing on the swings below. He had a long way to walk by himself—we saw him coming slowly with a blank face—he did the last bit more quickly with a little smile, and she kissed him. He hardly spoke the rest of the day but seemed a little bit pleased(?). Mrs Willcox went to find Sam. We saw them returning a long way off, Sam looking very puny, holding Mrs Willcox's hand and saying, 'Is that Karen?' Mrs Willcox let go of his hand, and he walked the last few steps alone till Mrs Hopgood picked him up and kissed him. She was near tears. Mrs Willcox and I left them on their own for a few minutes. Mrs W herself thought it best for the boys to return today if they're going to at all (it is more confusing otherwise) so I rang Miss Gibbs for permission, and went out to tell Mrs Hopgood. She looked happy and said, 'Lovely.' The children were sitting in a row on the wall, Sam with his arm round Karen, still asking, 'Is this Karen?'

We had lunch there and arranged various practical details. I'd been told beforehand how helpful the staff would be, and they certainly were. Mrs Willcox thinks both children have benefited in some ways by their four and a half weeks in care, and that Sam has been 'half-tamed'—to the optimum amount. He's been popular there. He ran into the staff-room without knocking while I was there, and was persuaded to knock on his way out. Mrs Willcox is a comfortable person (not hankering after her ear-rings). I'm less impressed by Mr Willcox, not knowing whether his manner is meant to be rude or casual, or both. At one point, when I was standing in the hall with Keith, Mr W approached, copying Keith's timidity, and saying, 'I'm as quiet as a mouse.' Then he suddenly jumped, which made a startling noise on the wooden boards. Keith stared at him with round eyes, and I felt it was the last thing to do with such a child, who is anti-man as it is.

Anyway we left very pleasantly, with the three children in the back of the car, and a big box of clean clothes in the boot. The boys were easier on this journey than when Mr Ripley and I took them to Redlands. Sam didn't give the same almost animal screams of excitement, and he only twice expected passing cars to crash. Mrs Hopgood kept turning round to talk to him. She and I talked a lot both ways, and went over things more thoroughly than we might otherwise have done. You can't feel reproachful when you actually meet her, though she is obviously plausible—to herself too, I expect. I'm not impressed when a person says, 'I've learnt my lesson—the hard way, but I've learnt it', but it's futile to reply 'Good', or 'Are you really sure?', in the same way that it's impossible to keep tackling Carol about stealing. I did tell her that we (or another agency) would like to visit her in future, and explained why. 'I should be pleased to be visited', she said.

Clearly there is nothing to be gained, but rather lost, by putting her through the mill deliberately. It struck me that the children will 'bring this home' to her as much as anybody. On the face of it, they were wonderful in their acceptance of her with no direct reproaches—but she was considerably smitten by the signs of their confusion. At first they often called her 'auntie'. 'You'll have to stop that', she said gently, 'I'm Mummy.' She told me it gives her 'a real jab' when Karen keeps asking 'Where's mummy?' This is because Mr Hopgood's sister, who kept Karen throughout, encouraged Karen to call her mummy. I heard her doing it, and remarked now that it was wrong. (Indeed I think it was consciously cruel.) This is the sort of thing Mrs H has to bear from her in-laws although they are endlessly helpful to Mr H and the children.

In the midst of all the comings and goings, Mrs Hopgood senior (over 60) has quietly married the man for whom she was house-keeping. No wonder she didn't leap to Miss Gibbs's suggestion of giving up her job to look after her son and grandchildren. I passed on a few things to Mrs Hopgood that Mrs Willcox had told me about the boys—nice things, reflecting well on her previous care, which pleased her. During the last part of the journey, Keith and Karen slept. But Sam was determined to get his bearings (unlike Keith, who's beyond asking). He questioned his mother for a long time, asking some questions several times in succession:

'Did you go on your holidays?'

'Well . . . kind of . . . .'

'What kind of?'

'Well, it wasn't a very nice holiday. . . .'

'What place we going now? Your place?'

'Yes, our place—you'll see when you get there. . . .'

'Are we going Auntie's place?'

'No, our place.'

'Is Daddy Auntie's place?'

'No, our place.'

'Is this Karen?'

'Yes, you know Karen. . . .'

'Where's Auntie Pat?' (one of Mrs H's friends who 'led her astray').

'You won't be seeing her any more. . . .'

Mrs Hopgood kept voicing her future intentions as if to make them more concrete. Eventually Sam relapsed into a contented silence. Then he began to sniff deeply and finally announced with great satisfaction: 'I smells tractor.' She obviously enjoys him. Mr Hopgood was out shopping when we reached their home—buying extra food, we thought, in case the boys returned. This seemed a happyish, satisfying sort of day to me, though exhausting. I got back to the office about 4.00 p.m. and did nine CHA Forms for Keith and Sam's discharge from care—unfortunately putting my initials by mistake in the square reserved for CO (Mr Tasker) which amused Miss Gibbs who is beginning to work herself up, wittily, for an advanced casework course.

In the evening I went to Andersham for another adoption welfare visit on Carmen's behalf. I plan to have visited about four times in the three months pre-court supervision stage (which is

up the day I leave) and still felt a bit vague about what I'm supposed to do here. Anyway I intended this evening to meet Mr
Hicks, who's been at work previously, and then try to reach more
brass-tacks in at least one more talk with Mrs Hicks. It turned
out to be a particularly comprehensive interview because Mr
Hicks was over an hour late in returning from work, and Mrs
Hicks let her hair down meanwhile, having protested that everything was fine hitherto.

She is adopting largely because she dreads another difficult
pregnancy and confinement, and is a bit guilty about this, so in a
way there is something positive about having parallels to pregnancy and labour in the long-drawn-out adoption procedure
culminating in court. We had a natural opportunity this time to
discuss basic things, such as telling Carmen later she is adopted,
and feelings about the natural mother connected with explana-
tions to Carmen, and how even 'own children' have fantasies
about parents, linked up with their 10-year-old son, Leslie, and
her difficulties in telling him about sex. She said, 'I remember
clearly when I was a child I used to sit on the door-step wrapped
in a red shawl because I wanted to make sure I was different. . . .'

The earlier indications about Leslie are beginning to tie up a
little—he does seem to have been a pretty-girlish sort of boy. They
always wanted a baby girl and would have called Leslie 'Miranda'
(a combination of their own names, Miriam and Andrew) but it
is to be Carmen's second name now. Leslie used to love dolls and
has recently started taking them to bed with him again, and he's
revived another old custom of going into Mr and Mrs Hicks's bed
with Carmen on waking in the morning. In fact I think Leslie is
well able to cope, being independent during his favourite out-door
activities, and that this is a thoroughly sane family with plenty of
room for quirks. Mr Hicks looks a little effeminate too, with one
of those painfully prominent Adam's apples. Carmen continues
to thrive. It's difficult discussing her slightly uncertain future
with the Hicks, and one can hardly conceive of the unlikely event
of her being removed from them—though they are bound to feel
it's on the cards until the Adoption Order is made.

Something that strikes me about the Marlshire Children's
Department is that their fieldworkers operate with a view to
maintaining their cases on a fairly even keel, and this does actually
seem to happen in practice. I do my work with the very same aim

but am never surprised, or not much, when people break out in unexpected ways.

29 July

I wrote frantically in the office all day, just breaking off to chat with visiting fieldstaff and students. I phoned Mrs Tolley about Carol—the compromise (?) I reached with Miss Farrar, having also talked to Mrs Willcox at Redlands about this missing jewellery again. The thing seems to be dying down—Carol hasn't mentioned it to Mrs Tolley. Otherwise the Tolley family are settling surprisingly well with Carol, exceeding our highest hopes although we're prepared for later upsets. Carol is mad on horses (a strange phenomenon in teenage girls, which sometimes stops once they get interested in boys) and Mr Tolley may be going to buy a young pony for her at the local autumn fair.

The three Collingham students came into our headquarters office for a prolonged visitation from their university tutor—they seem to mind more than we do. It's certainly true that children in an institution become 'ripe for leaving' and, in not quite the same way, I'm feeling very ripe now to stop being a student. What is particularly nice this time is being free to go on your way, without being pushed.

2 August

A.m. I went to Drayton to see Mrs Almond and Eamon. She was looking after two of her grandchildren for the morning—they were completely under her thumb and made to take a very quiet back seat while I was there. Mrs Almond apologized for being so preoccupied last Wednesday when I called—it turns out that she's had Miss Murphy, Shaun (the younger son, aged 7) and Shaun's private foster-mother, Miss Murphy's sister, under her own roof for a week! Miss Murphy was living with her sister in Drayton who is now separated from her husband, and they sought refuge with Mrs A whilst looking for a flat. Their cat and white mouse, whose habits turn Mrs A's stomach, are living in the garden shed.

Mrs Almond is half elated at having come up trumps and half genuinely worn out. I heard about the effect it is having on the various parties, as she sees it. The relationship between Mrs A and Miss M must have eased a little for this to happen at all, but is likely to remain complicated I think. Miss M is 'using' Mrs A at present but is not 'really grateful'—on the other hand, poor Miss M is receiving daily homilies. I realize more and more that Mrs A is a powerful person in her own way, and I don't doubt she'll come out on top of this immediate crisis. Meanwhile she is really shocked by the spoilt behaviour of Shaun (who wasn't brought up by her) and is having nightly battles to cure his enuresis. She tells his mother, 'You pull one way and your sister the other, and he wets the bed because his little mind is full of resentment. . . .' I agreed to some extent (while intrigued to imagine urine spurting from a little mind) and Mrs A replied a bit sharply, 'Yes, you've read this up in books and I've learnt from years of personal experience, so we both know. . . .'

Eamon frankly admits he's jealous of the extra attention Shaun receives from their mother, so 'a lot has come out in the open'. I saw Eamon, who seems to be surviving although I noticed traces of his old supercilious manner. He showed me his school report, which I'd been foolishly eager to see—hoping it would give a more definite indication of whether things really are a bit better. In fact it is very little better than last term's report—he has gone up two places in the exams. The most striking aspect is that what was his lowest mark last term is now his highest—Religious Instruction was 15 per cent and is now 60 per cent!

I reminded Mrs Almond as I was going that I'm leaving at the end of August. 'Where are you . . . but no, that's very rude of me.' I told her I'm going to south Loamshire, and received an invitation to visit afterwards. She picked a red rose from her garden and presented it with a little speech to me. (Miss Murphy may not have received my letter asking for another meeting—I'll make one more attempt after she's left Mrs A's again, and otherwise will write instead.)

Most of the afternoon was taken up with telephoning out and in about the Chubb family of Crossbridge. This is what had happened: the whole household flitted during the night of 22 July in the car bought by Gary 'out of his pocket money'. Later this broke down, and they transferred to a stolen car. For ten days they lived and slept in a car: Mrs Chubb and her three cohabitees (Gary aged 18, and two other men with prison records), the three little girls Linda, Susan and Tracey, and the baby, Jayne, born on 12 April when the children came into short-stay care. Each of the four adults slept with a child on his or her lap—which rather impresses me. It's a bit like the Dartmoor prisoner who hatched a bird's egg in his armpit. The men broke in and stole food as necessary.

When the first car broke down, they returned to Mrs Chubb's council house in Crossbridge to find that the locks had been changed—at this point they must have panicked again, and flitted in the stolen car. They were picked up by the police in north Loamshire on Bank Holiday Monday. The three men are now in prison and likely to have eighteen-month sentences. Mrs Chubb and the four children spent one night last night in a centre for homeless families. (This kept the Loamshire department busy in that area and I heard from one of my fellow-students that she and another colleague had bathed the children because the regular staff were off duty.) Today Mrs Chubb and children were returning to Crossbridge by train. Mr Worth (NSPCC Inspector) wanted the children removed immediately on arrival to a Place of Safety, which is what most of the telephoning was about.

It looked as though I would have to stay in the office during the evening to go on phoning, but I decided at 4.30 p.m. that it would be preferable to be on the spot. It was Inspector Worth's pigeon, but I thought I'd like to meet the family again (as I'd have liked to keep them on before) and that it might be pleasanter for the little girls if I were there when they were removed from their mother as they already know me, and had enjoyed being fostered, and also I had no experience of Place of Safety Orders. I reached Crossbridge station at 5.00 p.m. to find that Mr Worth had just met them off the train. I followed them to a local doctor's surgery and met them all there in Mr Worth's car, which was standing in the sun, causing an overpowering stench to rise.

They remembered me, and the girls started right from where we'd left off by reminding me of their foster-homes, and of how they'd played with Trudi. Mrs Chubb shows little but weariness and is more withdrawn as you'd expect. She just sat nursing the baby, and seemed not to realize its pitiful state. The girls looked little the worse (physically) for their adventure—I still think there are advantages in being reared in this sort of 'problem family'. But I was shocked to see the baby. I saw her the day after she was born and agreed then with the ward sister that it was an unusually fine, healthy baby. Her birth-weight was 8 lb and she can't be much more than that now, with thin arms and legs and a sickening skin colour like anaemic piglets. The incongruous thing (and most horrible) is that she still looks like a new baby, except for having this last three and a half months' experience showing in her face.

After some delay we all trooped into the surgery. It was a young woman doctor who'd had no experience of this sort of situation either. She examined them, and I think was hard put to it to testify that the three girls were being treated 'in a manner likely . . .', but she did eventually. Apparently Mr Worth only takes people to court as a very last resort (this is his first case for twelve months in the area) and the children had to go somewhere, as they now have no home. Then he drove the family to the next town to get a magistrate's signature, and met me later at his Marlford office, while I rang up the Places of Safety—Redlands for the three little girls, and a nursery in Marlford for Jayne, who will need expert nursing care (though she might have got it more naturally in a foster-home).

Mr Worth took over two hours to get a statement from Mrs Chubb in his front room while Mrs Worth and I looked after the children in the back room. After 9.00 p.m. we began thinking about moving the children. He slipped away quietly with Mrs Chubb and the baby, without the three girls seeing their mother to say goodbye. Having delivered the baby, he was going to try to persuade the maternal grandmother in Pilbury to take in Mrs Chubb for a time, and he is working towards her being put on probation with rehabilitative training as a requirement, hoping to reunite her with her children when possible. His wife and I took Linda, Susan and Tracey to Redlands—Mrs Willcox says she won't be sorry when I leave!

On the journey to Redlands, the girls sat in the back of my car, wearing gay paper hats on top of their filthy, ragged clothes, attention-seeking but full of joie de vivre—although a car can hold few charms for them by now. They jumbled all we told them of Redlands with their previous foster-homes and the fairy-stories Mrs Worth had been telling them. All they hoped for was something to eat before being put to bed. On the way back, Mrs Worth told me a lot about their arduous work with the NSPCC—she can't help envying Mrs Chubb with five children (the eldest with his grandmother in Pilbury) when she herself desperately wants more than one child. On reaching their house, we saw Mr Worth for a few minutes—he'd fixed Mrs Chubb up with her mother, and she's expecting me to visit her soon, and take her to see the children. I got to bed after midnight and found later that I'd got fleas but they seem to have gone of their own accord.

3 August

I made an early visit to Mrs Nash in Rickerton before she went out to work, to explain that her application to become foster-mother to her great-niece (Yvonne, at present in London in the care of East Dowling) is now approved. We made final arrangements for Mrs Nash to bring Yvonne back here at the end of her (Mrs N's) week's holiday in London on 13 August. Mrs Nash is a fairly young, dashing 'great-aunt' and, though she is most anxious to care for Yvonne, she evidently doesn't intend to lose a moment's pleasure in London over it. She has too full a programme to meet Yvonne's present foster-mother in the south suburbs, and will simply meet Yvonne at the station for the return journey to Rickerton, as she has 'an urgent appointment at the Houses of Parliament' that day.

It's an odd business altogether. East Dowling seems to have the main aim of returning Yvonne to Marlshire willy nilly. I keep having to write them supposedly educative letters, asking strings of questions about the underlying attitudes of the various people concerned—the separated parents, the man her mother is living with, her brother, her present foster-home ... and am told to administer the odd 'slap' to the East Dowling children's officer—for example: 'Mrs Nash said she had heard from you about your plans, which would seem something of a risk while her application was still under consideration. . . .' The person we continue to hear nothing of is Yvonne herself, who experienced two foster-home breakdowns as a result of her disturbed behaviour in Marlshire five years ago—and until we know something more definite, I can only try to prepare Mrs Nash in terms of adolescence generally. I shall overlap with Yvonne for only a fortnight, but she may well prove a headache to Miss Beckwith later, who seems to have the most hectic time in her sub-area.

I quite enjoy the different sorts of letter one has to write, varying from the very simple ones to semi-literate people from oneself, to these edifying ones I write in Mr Tasker's name. I find it difficult to put opinions into his mouth which he hasn't actually voiced, but he tells me he dislikes 'the Royal we' (which I tend to use in order to convey what I hope is the joint view of the boss and his student social worker).

The rest of the day was spent in the office. Supervision with Miss Farrar focused on where I have got to and what remains to be done in the next three weeks. I don't have to do more than I can over the meeting between Joe and Mrs Victor and Joe's mother, Mrs Kemp. Miss Gibbs also discussed with me how far I'm to co-operate with Inspector Worth over the Chubb family, and I'm learning to distinguish between removals to a Place of Safety and voluntary receptions into care—all the same it meant doing sixteen CHA forms for the Chubb children.

My course-tutor (as distinct from personal tutor) visited in the afternoon, and I was able to show her Exhibit A—Mrs Almond's red rose blooming on my desk. She looked at the records of this case since her last visit—it took a very obvious turn for the better from 17 May when Mr Tasker visited Mrs Almond with me, and through my discussing the situation at the university. I don't know how it might have been different if it had remained my 'most burning case'. I haven't really been at grips with it since tackling the religious issue in a way which seemed appropriate to *me*. Much of my effort over this seems to have consisted of digging my toes in obstinately, and the net result is nothing very tangible. All one can say is that the case has come alive after nearly twelve years, and that I've met all the people concerned (except Miss Murphy's sister and Shaun), and that we know them and their likely reactions a bit better, and have made some compromises, and tried to make some investments for the future. I'm told I can at least wear the feather of Eamon's examination mark in Religious Instruction changing from 15 to 60 per cent!

4 August

This morning I suddenly decided to go to the back of beyond (Jacob's Ladder) to see the woodcutter family, and whether the two older boys have arrived from Scotland and are settling with their father and step-mother here. The roads were busy, and I remembered on the way that I had an appointment with Mr Tasker back in Marlford at 2.00 p.m. so I drove nearly a hundred miles as fast as possible, and had less than ten minutes' interview with Mrs McTavish in between. It was enough though to finish my responsibility in the case, having caught a glimpse of the boys in the flesh, and hearing from Mrs McTavish of their arrival and settling and the interplay of all parties including the Scottish grandparents, and seeing that the door-step is weeded. The family may crop up again later but are all right at the moment. I spun out the very short interview into two pages of a report, and sent copies to our relevant area office and Cameronshire children's department.

2.00 p.m.—discussed Erika and the Strickland family with Mr Tasker, feeling a bit disturbed about the time lag here, though it seems inevitable. He appeared to accept my view of the situation, which I'd have thought harder to swallow than my interview with Father O'Sullivan, as it's such a starkly exaggerated case. It must often be difficult for the head of an organization to give official blessing when he hasn't seen the 'facts' except on paper, through the eyes of a fieldworker. Anyway, it's agreed that I should first approach the child guidance clinic; that we see the possibility of Erika needing to be received into (or committed to) care later; that I should report to our opposite numbers in Germany, who are Erika's legal guardians, and who may prefer her to be in their care, if it comes to this; and I'm to consider how to refer and hand over the case to child guidance.

Later I telephoned Miss Onslow, psychiatric social worker— she sounds interested and agrees to try, but August is a difficult month for her. She is willing to visit until the psychiatrist can see Erika and Mrs Strickland in September, but cannot take responsibility if the situation explodes meanwhile. We are to discuss it again when she's read the report (which isn't typed yet). On the other hand, Mr Tasker says he can't take responsibility unless Erika is committed through the court. There is talk of my continuing to visit until I leave, but I can't see that this is much help if it's anything like my first interview there, or that it's much advantage to Miss Onslow in taking over.

In the evening I visited the Hopgood family in Rickerton—just a week after Keith and Sam came home. Sam, who loves cars, greeted me with the words, 'I'm not coming in your car!' I told him I didn't want to move him again, that I'd just come to see them. I didn't stay long because the children couldn't be sure what I was up to, and I think it would take several visits before the family could accept me on this new basis and recover from previous associations. They don't want anything definite from us now, and Mrs Hopgood is vulnerable in a different way now she's got the children home. She looked tired, ill and dispirited after a week of doing her duty as a housewife, and her manner with the children is sharper than a week ago—which seems genuine enough and natural.

Keith was as free as I've ever seen him—which isn't saying much. Mrs Hopgood told me the only two small problems she says she has at the moment, and gathered up her social poise at the end to say she looks forward to my coming again. We shall have to decide who is to visit in future. The local health visitor, who knows them well and with whom I've been in touch throughout, might be the best person, but I do think the family needs a lot of support indefinitely and that our department must at least keep a close link if similar breakdowns are to be avoided in future.

5 August

All day in the office. The person who normally does my typing is away, and I couldn't leave the Chubb social history much longer, so typed six copies this afternoon and got them off to the various bodies, and we shall still need six more copies next week. Also typed half Erika's report which I'm anxious to get off but hadn't time to finish. The office staff were different again as they saw me typing—and so slowly too. The other person in the room was nearly frantic about some work she was doing for Mr Tasker as she couldn't decipher his rough notes. I, as a student, might have 'buzzed through' to ask him, but as typists we seemed unable to do more than stare at the worst words with our heads turned at all angles, ask other people, and look up possible words in the dictionary.

8 August

A.m. in the office—half an hour late after having a puncture on the way. East Dowling children's department has been stung into activity at last, and sent a report answering most of the questions about Yvonne and her recent family and fostering situation, before she moves to Mrs Nash in Rickerton.

Most of the morning was spent in finishing Erika's report, plus typing a letter to the German authorities, asking for their opinion should there be any question of Erika's committal to care later. Before lunch I took Miss Onslow's copies round to the child guidance clinic, as there seemed to have been more than enough delay already, and papers are prepared to hover indefinitely (I think, though their mass movement is swift in fact) between other people's in- and out-trays. Miss Onslow read it while I was there and discussed it. We decided that I'll do one or two more visits soon. She will start visiting at the end of next week. She'd have liked me to visit the school had it not been holiday time, so she will send out their form asking for comments next term. I'd been asked to reiterate Mr Tasker's point about our not being responsible unless Erika is referred via court. I said I'd send copies of any further reports, and left—much relieved.

In the afternoon I went to Long Winkley to see Mrs Ethel Rock, really in reply to her letter of thanks at the end of May. I just saw Stephen (Mrs Gladys Rock's adopted son) as I passed through the village. Mrs Ethel was pleased to see me and recounted her immediate family news, including Jenny's private fostering and how successful it had been, and her own op. and convalescence. She had little news of her sisters the other side of Marlford except through the rent man, and seems to exchange news with Mrs Gladys through the latter's husband 'Perce' when he comes to deliver bread. I asked whether, if Jenny should need care away from home in future, Mrs Ethel would be willing for her sister-in-law, Mrs Gladys, to undertake it. She would, and Mrs Gladys has already offered. So it was worth visiting, apart from wanting to meet Mrs Ethel again. Another time in future, it's quite likely that Mrs Ethel would apply for care to the children's department again, and might have fallen out with Mrs Gladys once more in the meantime. So even if this happens, it's worth knowing that an outsider can probably arrange things between both women in order for Jenny to be cared for within the family.

Then I went to Pilbury to see Erika's mother, Mrs Strickland. Erika came to the door and explained that her mother was out for the afternoon and evening. She told me in careful English when

I'd be likely to find her mother in. I said how very well she speaks English—her face lit up, and we had quite a long conversation on the doorstep. She said she hadn't picked up this new language from her mother—'My friends learnt me.' She didn't know whether or not she'd regretted leaving Germany, and could only say with sad pride, 'I didn't cry.' Her young half-sister Rosa emerged at one point, and made a mischievous reference to the fact that Erika must still go to bed at 7.30 with her, even though their mother was out. Erika told her with detached tolerance to go indoors and finish her tea. She was a different child today—freer and more natural—even her appearance less tragically dramatic. I wondered whether I'd made my first visit on a particularly fraught afternoon, or whether it's always liable to be like that when the family is together. Later on, while I was still in Pilbury I saw Erika skipping out of a grocer's shop.

I called at Mrs Chubb's mother's cottage in Pilbury, but found only her brother at home. On returning later, I hardly recognized Mrs Chubb. Now she is washed and in cleaner clothes, it's apparent that she's lost considerable weight since April and has become thoroughly worn down. Her eldest child, Dean (aged 6), lives there with his grandmother, and took a large share of the conversation. He is like Linda to look at and I don't know what he thinks about being permanently away from his immediate family. Mrs Chubb listened most attentively to all Dean's and her 15-year-old brother's remarks. She's a nice change from some mothers one meets—hopeless in material ways, but rather good (I think) otherwise. We talked about her four children in Places of Safety and arranged to go together to Redlands to visit the three little girls next Tuesday. Her brother said he'd have liked to come too, 'because they're my nephews, you see', only he is due back at his approved school. Dean begged to come with us, 'because I likes Linda, Susan and Tracey', so he is coming too.

9 August

In the afternoon I set out on a widespread round of calls in mid and west Marlshire. I had an appointment to see Joe's mother, Mrs Kemp, in Cranbury at 3.00 p.m. She'd written only this morning asking me to come at 3.00 'because it's the best time for us to talk privately'. I had gathered from the administrator who collects her financial contribution for Joe that, although her second husband knows about Joe, any mention of him constitutes a real threat to the marriage. So I was all set to be very discreet, and was amazed on entering the door of their attractive cottage to find Mr Kemp looming large at the kitchen table. I could hardly introduce myself, and left it to Mrs K to start the ball rolling.

Mrs Kemp invited me into the front room and asked her husband to come too. We all sat down and went hammer and tongs for three quarters of an hour. (At the end I still didn't know who we were supposed to be being private from—and can only imagine that Mrs Kemp had had a fleeting wish to meet Joe secretly and then thought better of it, or that Mr K changed his shift at the last minute.) By the end I liked them both very much. Mrs Kemp is in complete contrast to Gregory's mother, Mrs White, whom I like too. She isn't 'blowsy' or 'coarse' as Joe's foster-mother Mrs Victor pictured her, but is something like a white version of Mrs Victor herself (only I shan't tell Mrs V so), being an extraordinarily capable, pleasant and strong-minded woman who has attained a measure of happiness after a hard background.

Mr Kemp, strangely enough, though he has no 'touch of the tar-brush', is rather negroid in his features with a powerful physique. He was tough and truculent in this preliminary interview. They simply knew that Joe had reached a stage when he is likely to want to know something of his parentage, and they couldn't see why this should suddenly be so. Mr Kemp started by saying they have two children of their own (aged 11 and 3) 'and if anything happens in this business to upset my children, I'll be upset, and the marriage will be upset, so you (to Mrs Kemp) can make your mind up, but if anything happens to upset my children I'll be upset, and. . . .' He went on in this groove for some time, and Mrs K was equally voluble. She obviously has more mixed feelings, and is desperately keen to do 'the right thing', but dreads dragging up her past.

I explained more about the present position, and how Joe's older foster-brother had recently met his mother. This meant nothing to them because they thought Joe would have a different temperament anyway. On hearing about Joe, Mrs Kemp volunteered that she has the same happy-go-lucky, wild streak but cannot believe Joe doesn't also possess her persistence. Both Mr and Mrs Kemp felt that, in Joe's shoes, they wouldn't be content with just one meeting, or with occasional meetings away from Cranbury. They realize such a meeting could be held in controlled circumstances while Joe is still in care, but they still dread his finding the way to their home, or demanding to be taken 'home'. It eased them a little to hear that Mrs Victor is reluctant about a meeting, and that Joe is very much at home with her. Mrs Kemp grasped at this, saying that, if Joe is happy, it's best all round not to disturb him.

Mr Kemp offered that he and his wife should meet Mrs Victor on her own with me (which I'd been going to suggest) but thought better of the idea as soon as he'd voiced it. I produced Miss Farrar's trump card about Joe perhaps turning up on their door-step suddenly, having made his own enquiries after he is discharged from care at 18. Mr Kemp, very heated, asked me, 'What could you do then, eh? What could you *do*?' I asked, 'What *could* you do?' He found it unanswerable but both he and Mrs Kemp explained that they would prefer to face this hurdle alone if it ever happened, rather than deliberately encourage a meeting which they couldn't follow through sincerely but only in a spirit of fear and unwillingness. They moved into this neighbourhood about a year ago and have worked hard to build up their home. Through the risk of losing all this and because she cannot see purpose in meeting Joe, Mrs Kemp finally decided not to see him. She didn't ask much about him and evidently preferred not to know. It seems this is a second marriage for both of them—he said something about a wife deserting him with a child he had never seen.

Before I could begin to sympathize that he is in the same boat as Mrs Kemp, in that they both have an unknown child of their own, Mr Kemp suddenly closed the meeting and suggested we adjourn for a cup of tea. Back in the other room he showed quite a different side of himself, especially after he'd removed sticking-plaster from his thumb and was alarmed to find it white underneath. While we had tea their two daughters skipped in and out, very friendly, and Mr Kemp is obviously devoted to them. I sat in the armchair with two symbolic kittens—one pure black, the other equally white—and heard more about Mr and Mrs Kemp's recent life together. He said he could tell I'd been a farmer (as he is, part-time) as soon as I'd walked in the door—though I shouldn't have thought it was at all obvious myself. He became light-hearted and amusing, and Mrs K fitted in, so the last half was enjoyable.

Mrs Kemp walked down the field-path with me when I left, and shook off the children by the final gate so that we had a private word by my car. She said, not far off tears, that the situation is hard either way, but repeated that it's best to leave it as it is. I agreed, and asked if she could possibly tell me something of Joe's father, to pass on to Joe later if he asks. She told me the little she knew, and concluded, 'It would really be better if Joe traced his father than me—with the colour, you know. . . .' She last heard of him in London, 'But I couldn't follow him there—I hadn't the money in those days never mind anything else. . . .' 'And will you thank his foster-mother very much from me for all she's done ?' She said formally but warmly that she hoped she'd meet me again. I said I thought it unlikely this side of heaven. She seemed to find this quite satisfactory, and waved me off with a mixture of friendliness and relief.

(I might have known that Miss Farrar, on first hearing briefly about it, would like me to visit again, but I cannot see what for. The Kemps and I discussed it thoroughly once, and came to a genuine decision apparently. They are paying contributions for Joe so have shown what responsibility they could. I daresay, after several more visits, one could persuade Mrs Kemp to meet Joe secretly without her husband's knowledge. She won't change her mind otherwise. It is impressive that she and her husband could meet me together, and I'm sure they feel there was only this one occasion to rise to. More interviews would cause extra strain, and secret meetings would be an intolerable strain to Mrs Kemp. Mrs Victor doesn't want a meeting, and Joe doesn't particularly want one at present—so. Miss Farrar and I both think it would be worth my writing to Mrs Kemp to ask if she'd let me have an old photo of herself which could be given to Mrs Victor to give to Joe when he asks. So I think I shall just write.)

The positive aspects arising from this interview seem to be:

(a) A definite decision has been made which suits the people concerned. Joe, unlike Gregory, is thought not to be the sort of person to whom a glimpse of his mother is vital.

(b) Much more is known about Joe's mother. There is virtually nothing in the records except that she is 40 and has married twice. I shall describe her as thoroughly as possible to Mrs Victor and to the supervising authority, Marlford City, so that Joe can be told, and retold in future.

(c) The best thing is that one can present a 'good' picture. This will be helpful to Joe and to Mrs Victor, who fears a hereditary weakness of character.

(d) Slight information about Joe's father—nothing was known before.

(e) The fact that Mr and Mrs Kemp have tried to understand Joe's position in all this, and that they wish him well, even though they cannot meet him.

Then I went on to Withydean, and asked for Gregory's mother at the hotel there. I'd hoped to fit her in while I was within twenty miles but she had gone off duty, so I had my hair cut instead, and will see her another time. I think Miss Farrar wants me to help her to tell her husband about Gregory, but I'm not sure about this. Some people 'come clean' automatically because they know from experience that they're nearly always found out. An overlapping group are those who confess because they're not happy otherwise, although it may put a burden on the other person. There are people extraordinarily capable of living with a guilty secret indefinitely. Mrs White may be one of them, or she and Mr White may be hiding their separate knowledge of Gregory and be greatly relieved to mention it at last.

Whatever happens, these white mothers are in a terrible position and they, by definition, have no personal colour-bar. I think if there were more time, it would be helpful for them to talk freely about it. I also think that someone who isn't saddled with a secret coloured son can't try to persuade someone who is to do what the former thinks best. People have their own ways of meeting their own sufferings. It's the same in other situations when people are going through the mill. It makes me cross when a thorough-going 'extrovert' prods at an 'introvert' who will not blow his top or have a crying orgy, and vice versa. If one person is in a hell of a fix and the other isn't, the latter must respect to some extent the methods through which the former seeks to survive.

Some animals in difficulties keep very still; others roar and thrash about. A rabbit wouldn't say to an eel, 'For heaven's sake, freeze—it's a more normal reaction!' The same rabbit might have an outburst in different circumstances. Sometimes the herd (especially of cows) makes a concerted attack to kill an ill or injured member as if for the sake of self-protection (from disease) or inability to tolerate the unnatural. Not unsimilarly, it seems to me that human help is often disguised interference or selfishness. The 'introvert' would feel more comfortable if the other stopped crying, and the 'extrovert' less bewildered if the other broke down. But I think, if it isn't your own personal problem, you mustn't forcibly advocate your own recipe. The other may have resources that you know nothing of—he may have a punch-ball or a box of paper handkerchiefs in his bedroom.

If it's more painful to watch impotently, that is your problem, because there is a limit to the potential bearing of other people's burdens. Suffering is primitive and private, and it is arrogant to pretend that it can be shared completely in civilized cosiness. The afflicted person does need the help of other people, but usually gives some indication of the form in which this is most acceptable —and this is due to him while he is the more hardly hit. It would seem to be rare that would-be comforters are so close and empathetic that they genuinely feel quite as keenly as the actual sufferer (for them to say they do, can almost amount to a type of blackmail). It is more likely that the second person is affected directly by an aspect rather than by the whole of the other's problem.

For example, if Mr Kemp were honest he would say, 'I do sympathize with my wife, but I'm jealous that she once had sexual relations with a negro, and fearful lest my children and neighbours find out', rather than, 'I'm heartbroken that my wife is separated from her illegitimate coloured son.' He is mainly affected by his own jealousy and fear, unless he is an exaggerated Siamese twin to his wife's private emotions. Social workers who imply 'Do show a bit of decent feeling' or 'Don't show a bit of indecent feeling' are more likely to be considering themselves. The most you can do is to leave the other person free to show or not show according to his need, and remember that, unless the other is hysterically shallow (or numb) or escaping into a sea of 'neurotic' suffering which drowns the actual pain, you are in the humbler position of not minding quite so much. And until science has discovered a way (which it won't) of sticking a needle into somebody which registers so many sens of sensitivity, you have to take it that everybody feels things as least as much as you do.

Conversely, if you become overwhelmed by other people's troubles, you might either go hard, like some people's idea of a hospital nurse, or make a hash of filling in the forms which was perhaps the only practical means of helping open to you at that moment. A social worker had better look to her own inner tangles, and proper meals, sleep and recreation, before she falls into the blasphemy of trying to bear the world's burdens. If social workers could wave wands, the world would be chaotic—the more I think about it, the more certain I am that the most you can do is recognize yourself as a fellow human, and seek to work in harmony with, rather than against, energies and forces for growth within the other person. All this of course is only what I think ideally.

Anyway, having had my hair cut just before the shop closed, I went on next to Dencombe, to start looking for George's mother, Miss Gardiner. It isn't that she's hiding, but has moved recently without telling us her address. All Mrs Yates (George's foster-mother) knows is that the new house is called 'Dick Whittington'. I started by asking in confidence at the police station—they'd never heard of it but will make discreet enquiries before my next visit. On the way back, I passed what I recognized to be Miss Gardiner's old address. It was uninhabited, but a small notice in the window announced: For Sale—apply to Gardiner at Whitting Dean. This puts a new complexion on it. Even before, it looked as though Mrs Yates wasn't over-anxious for George to have much contact with his mother! She has battled in her own simple way over this for thirteen years, and has plenty of ammunition because Miss Gardiner 'doesn't behave very well' on the rare occasions when she does visit George.

I didn't know before this placement that the job included these tracing expeditions, and it's an aspect I quite enjoy. There is something satisfying in finding what was hidden or lost, and so far nobody has minded being found.

10 August

Miss Farrar, Miss Gibbs and I discussed what parts of my work will revert to the area team when I leave. Some of the work will be complete for the time being in this area—e.g. the McTavish woodcutter family, Erika; Gregory, Joe and Mrs Victor, and three adoption situations. The four children in the three basic foster-homes will go back to Mrs Garvey. Miss Beckwith will have the Chubb family, and the new adolescent foster-child, Yvonne, from

East Dowling with Mrs Nash—it has yet to be decided whether she and/or the health visitor will continue with the Hopgood family. We continued with a supervision session. Miss Farrar rarely makes a personal remark but said today she'd realized I reached a crescendo of scaredness about Mrs Almond at one point, and thought it valuable to have overcome this (although I've met much more frightening people in my time, but not as 'clients', and doubt whether Mrs A will be the last). I had a letter from Frances's mother, Mrs Stokes, this morning, getting worried because the new adoption certificate hasn't come through yet. It's a pity adoption is so complex in some ways, because it's concrete help over facts which people seek first.

In the afternoon I went to see Mrs Strickland in Pilbury. Erika opened the door but didn't speak today. Her mother felt at a disadvantage in a dressing-gown, but gave her positive feeling about Erika free rein this time when her husband was out. After I'd told her that the child guidance clinic has offered to help, and that Miss Onslow will be calling later next week, we talked about Erika for a few minutes. I heard that Erika is 'very nice sometimes' but 'a devil gets into her for hours at other times. . . .' 'If you had come this morning, you would have clasped your hands!' (In horror, I imagine.)

I said something to the effect that it had been courageous to bring Erika to England, and tried to appreciate Mrs Strickland's affection for Erika. She broke down completely into painful crying, saying, 'She is my child—I cannot give up my child.' If she cannot cope with Erika here, the child may have to return to her legal guardians in Germany, and Mrs Strickland also fears upsetting her own parents because she wouldn't agree to their having Erika again. For the next few minutes I couldn't speak without causing Mrs S to cry violently each time, and I was extra sorry because she was in a hurry to change and get off to her evening work. We finished by making sure she understands the referral to child guidance, and the functions of the two agencies, and looks forward to Miss Onslow, and then I left with good wishes.

Next I went to see Mrs Hopgood in Rickerton. It was a little easier than last week, and Mrs H is designing the pattern of these interviews herself at present. I go once a week; we sit down and she tells me the events of her week, as though she were somebody much younger. 'It's been quite a happy week. . . . I've been to the doctor . . . he's given me some pills to straighten out my stomach. . . . I think I'm going blind in this eye. . . . I'm getting on all right with Mr Hopgood—you know he said I wasn't to have anything to do with Mrs Winter, well she asked me to be friends again this week, but I said I can't not really—not like it was . . . I've taken up knitting—a jumper for myself next summer—ever such a pretty pattern. . . . I'm going to make things for the children next. . . . I went to the pictures last night. . . . I'm trying to clear our Clubs, and I'm going to start distempering downstairs. . . .'

I've got a theory about Mrs Hopgood. Sometimes if you look at a person ordinarily, it's almost impossible to see any wholeness behind their conflicting motivations—but, if you look at them with a special pair of spectacles, things seem to fit logically. If you look at Mrs Hopgood in the light of her being an ex-approved school girl, it does seem more coherent. I think her desertion was typical of an absconding—the rising tension leading up to it ('I don't know if you can understand, but everything had got so tight inside that I really had to run away'); her extreme irresponsibility while away, the way she went to her mother's and was disappointed yet again, her difficulty in coming back even when she wanted to, her distempering gestures towards punishment-cum-reparation, her assertions 'I've learnt my lesson the hard way' and 'I'm going to turn over a new leaf', her frequent voicing of her intentions hoping to make them come true, her craving for sympathy and attention even from people whom she feels are bound to disapprove.

The present interviews fit too, although it is different now there is no official aspect of the children being in care. I've noticed that ex-approved school girls, when they find themselves in a sticky situation afterwards, sometimes try to cope by reproducing bits of the framework they knew while in the school for the sake of security and support—whether it is very appropriate or not. I once visited a Downcroft girl, Jenny, who had absconded to London (never been there before) in the inadequate clothes she stood up in, without money, and who'd been doing domestic work for several weeks, posing as an agricultural student. As the headmistress didn't want Jenny back, I was sent to see if her circumstances seemed suitable for her to stay in London; she entertained me in an attic room, and I realized what an effort ordinary, outside life required when I saw that Jenny had pinned

123

on her wall her weekly budget, menu and timetable (unless she had simply displayed these for the purpose of my visit, in which case it was equally odd that she should think I'd expect to find such items in non-institutional life).

In much the same way, Mrs Hopgood is struggling to organize herself in the house, is purging her friends, is treating herself to a weekly outing at the cinema, is knitting to keep herself out of mischief, and so on. I gather that at Hawthorn Grange she was the sort of girl who manages to be 'good' in this limited environment, in order to earn the approval of staff, who welcome these withdrawn ones as leaven in the lump. I don't think one would want to encourage this pattern, but it is perhaps a necessary stage. Looking back, she has a rosy picture of Hawthorn Grange as the first place where she was happy. It isn't yet decided what form her support from social worker(s) will take in future; meanwhile I think it quite useful to take on the role she engineers. She needs someone to visit frequently just to listen to her account of her week's activities. It isn't enough for her to know inwardly what she is accomplishing—she must tell somebody so as to have her efforts appreciated in order to give her the heart to continue.

According to this pattern, Mrs Hopgood could accept quite a firm approach as it might feel safer at present. I shall only be visiting her twice more, but I wonder how one would try to develop this stage. One would hope, as the relationship grew more realistic, that her inner resources would grow and that her effort would emerge more naturally, without the present flavour of mechanical desperation which keeps her at a physically low ebb. (I hope this isn't distorting Mrs Hopgood for the sake of my own ex-residential pattern.)

11 August

During the morning I went to see Mrs Victor to tell her about my meeting two days ago with Joe's mother. I told her as much as possible and she was obviously relieved that Mr and Mrs Kemp don't want to be in touch with Joe. I also described Mrs Kemp as fully as possible. Mrs Victor listened closely and says she will pass this picture on to Joe as and when he asks. She agreed it would be helpful to have a photo too, if Mrs Kemp will provide one. I said I thought she'd be relieved to know that Mrs Kemp isn't 'weak' or 'coarse'—she replied emphatically, 'It's a great relief!' (but I think she is most relieved that Mrs K is likely to stay only a description). I told her what we know of Joe's father, and conveyed Mrs Kemp's message of thanks to Mrs Victor as Joe's foster-mother. She appeared most receptive and then closed the subject, saying, 'Dear Joe!'

I went on to ask whether she has heard from Gregory's mother, Mrs White. She said she hadn't heard a word; that Gregory has shown no further interest and is preoccupied with outdoor activities. However, she added that she has found the contact with Gregory's mother useful, because she can bring it up when his behaviour is awkward. He was moody last weekend, so 'I whipped him with it'—for example, by saying that she knew now that he could not have inherited these traits, implying that any moodiness is his own fault. It sounded as though she and Gregory had been at loggerheads for a day or two, and he climbed down completely when he could no longer stand her displeasure. I have long interviews with Mrs Victor—she tells me a lot about her colourful past life. Today we said a provisional goodbye; agreed that we'd enjoyed our meetings, and she (not I) said she thought the results had been beneficial to all concerned. She may travel to Barchester with me the day I leave here as she's wanting to spend a weekend there with one of her old foster-daughters who now has six children.

I'm realizing more and more that this colour project was an ambitious thing to try to tackle in so short a time. It really needed years of preparation with Mrs Victor alone, but she is accustomed to taking charge of events. She is so strong outwardly and vital that it would be difficult to reach her real feelings about her foster-children's white mothers. I didn't know until recently that she has made it impossible on past occasions for Gregory and Joe to meet their mothers. It is extra delicate when you're dealing with another authority's foster-home. The amount of guilt, possessiveness, rivalry and uncertainty involved makes it particularly difficult. It is basically the problem of reaching a balance between child, mother and foster-mother, but with the additional colour problem. Mrs Victor ignores the whole colour question, but she cannot really be oblivious of it. She builds up pictures of grasping white mothers demanding their sons home, rather than see that the mothers are disgraced in the eyes of some white people (especially in a conservative, rural area) and want to keep it dark. This must be painful to her and makes her subtly aggressive.

The general idea seems to be that a coloured foster-mother is the ideal solution to this problem, but it cannot be so to pure West Indian eyes any more than it is to us. Her foster-children are all shades—not black, white or good red herring—so the conflicts cannot be disposed of by relying entirely on Mrs Victor. Gregory and Joe, in adolescence, seem to be upsetting her in more ways than wanting to know about their backgrounds and beginning to grow away from her. I think it is better in the circumstances that Joe shouldn't meet his mother, and I hope the information about his parents will be enough for him later on.

It begins to look as though Gregory will wish he hadn't met his mother. It was left to Mrs Victor to support him, which she has done in a punishing sort of way, and it's doubtful now whether she or Gregory will encourage further meetings. I feel that his mother has been brought into this on somewhat false pretences. Mrs White seems unusually simple, innocent and undemanding, so that the relationship need not have been crippled with guilt and rivalry. She has faith in Mrs Victor; has asked for virtually nothing, and apparently won't receive much.

In the afternoon there was a county staff meeting and the room was filled by a gathering of the clans. The guest speaker was Mrs Merrill of the Marlford Adoption Society—the audience was quite moved by her entertaining enthusiasm. She has organized this voluntary society for several years and has received adoption selection and welfare supervision reports from our fieldworkers all this time. She knew the names but not many faces before. The fieldstaff were equally glad to know that their reports hadn't gone off into the blue—that Mrs Merrill finds them valuable, especially when she is in any doubt. She gave examples, one of which was my Hicks in Andersham with Carmen; when she saw from my report that the Hicks still hadn't received the mother's signed consent, she visited them to explain that the diocesan worker in that area usually takes a longish time, and she tried to hustle the worker.

12 August

I arrived in the morning to hear Miss Farrar on the telephone talking about Carol having 'run away' from the Tolleys the previous evening. Carol had taken two small amounts of money from Mrs Tolley, and had disappeared with a duck for company when challenged. I could just imagine her with this duck, and how she would credit it with human-plus sympathy and understanding. Mrs Tolley had coped very sensibly, and had been exasperated with relief when eventually Carol turned up, having hovered just out of reach on the premises while the whole family searched for her for four hours in rain and dark. Mrs Marren spent a long time there last night and today, and there is a general feeling now that the fostering situation has been successfully tested, and proved its sticking-power.

During the morning, Miss Farrar gave me three guesses as to who was wanting me on the telephone. It was Mrs Almond of Drayton, of course. She talked for half-an-hour non-stop in a trembly voice. There has been another blow-up; 'a lot has come out into the open', and Miss Murphy is discovered to be 'at the bottom of everything'. Mrs Almond has weathered the storm but it's left her very washed out. I can't begin to write down all the ins and outs. Mrs A has quite changed towards Miss Murphy's sister and her husband, who were separated. She has been successful in 'bringing husband and wife together' and has had several long talks with the husband, giving him much homely advice. '... and for God's sake, Dick (excuse me, Miss Sparrow—that wasn't swearing—I meant it in the nice way) *be* a husband in future and don't....' She has discovered that Miss Murphy's sister is a fellow-sufferer in privately fostering the younger son Shaun, and hasn't even been paid. Mrs A has begged the sister to demand payment, I imagine as an insurance to herself lest Eamon be removed to where payment isn't required, because Miss Murphy is complaining over the amount she has to pay Mrs A, and I think this is what makes Miss M desperate often.

Meanwhile Miss Murphy was turned out of Mrs Almond's house on her own, and was refused access to her sister's home where she'd been before—until she had a haemorrhage ('she knew she'd done wrong, you see') soon after raising merry hell at the sister's home, and they weakened and took her in. Mrs Almond told Eamon, 'I'm sorry Son, but I couldn't put up with your mum any longer....' He replied, 'That's all right, she asked for it. I heard her coming in at all hours, and dressing up like a young girl, when she's *my mum*....' Mrs Almond was horrified by this ('I don't know what's going on in his little mind') and gave Eamon a lecture about respecting his mother, which must have been bewildering.

Mrs A told me that one result of this upheaval had been 'a most unpleasant incident'. Eamon and two or three other boys had played one evening behind the RC Church, and had thrown hard apples and even stones at the windows of Father O'Sullivan's house. Fortunately Fr O'Sullivan has been 'very very sweet', and Mrs Almond is footing the repair bill. She asked me whether she should show the bill to Miss Murphy 'as proof of what a mother can do to her son'. My instinct was to say no—it couldn't do anything except hurt Miss M, and Mrs A herself must realize the incident is very near the RC bone. Miss Murphy is talking wildly of dumping both Eamon and Shaun in Ireland this October. Mrs Almond says this is only a fraction of what she's found out—she would like me to visit next week to hear the whole story. 'Goodbye Pet—forgive me, dear—I get so used to talking to the children but I only meant it in the nice way.' I was quite glad the others could only hear me murmuring on the receiving end. She wants me to discuss what can be done, but thinks 'we can only continue hoping for the best'—and I agree.

After she'd rung off, I had a long inward laugh about the old Adam in Eamon throwing apples from the tree of knowledge of good and evil at Father O'Sullivan's windows, and then began trying to reconstruct the monologue on paper. I had a momentary temptation to suppress the apple incident, as I do not want to spend my final fortnight supposedly straightening out the feelings of all parties about it, and at first sight it looks as if the last state of this religious problem is worse than the first. It's certainly finished with a bang. But I hope it did Eamon a power of good, and I shall stress the idea that this is much healthier than the night terrors he was having in the spring term. (It turns out that Miss Farrar is delighted! That is her saving grace in more than one sense: however impossible her initial plans seem for me and my families, she is nearly always satisfied even when something vastly different happens.)

At 12.30 I called for Inspector Worth and drove him to Redlands for the case conference. It was to be an unusually full afternoon with more people present, so the meeting was held in a larger room with seating planned to let fieldstaff come and go quickly after introducing their cases. The Chubb family was first on the agenda; Inspector Worth, workers from probation, mental welfare, and maternal and child (medical) welfare had come for this. I was expecting to report back on the Hopgoods but not to introduce the Chubbs, only it happened the other way round. All parties added their piece to a discussion of the Chubb family lasting three quarters of an hour. A new factor is that Mrs Chubb is discovered to be even less intelligent than her young partner, Gary (so their 'combined IQ' is much less than 120). Apparently her mother refused special schooling for her, and she was under a form of voluntary supervision until this petered out years ago. Everyone seems to agree there is much positive about Mrs Chubb's care of her children, and that we should aim at probation including a period of residential training with as many of her children as possible, leading to their reunion in a house found by the co-ordinating officer or the NSPCC. The children may be committed to care, but with every intention of returning them home.

Gary has a six-month prison sentence for the stolen car, and is not going to be brought into this neglect case. The mental welfare officer was encouraged to get him into an institution if possible. All the other parties think it would be fatal for him and Mrs Chubb to live together again, and seem willing to move heaven and earth on Mrs C's behalf—on condition that they remain apart. I think it might be more realistic to include Gary in the plans—it seems more than a casual affair and they were thinking of divorce and marriage last April. It's fantastic for officials to imagine that Mrs C will go on for very long without picking up some man—it's as natural to her as breathing—so I think it might as well be Gary and that they could be assisted together as a team. Mrs Chubb does seem to have lovely children whoever the father is, and their intelligence (though lower than average) is higher than hers.

Mr and Mrs Willcox spoke about Linda, Susan and Tracey—they cannot help being impressed by the natural gaiety of these three; their lack of fear and their close bond with their mother. Mrs Willcox said the only trouble is that I'm wanting to bring their mother to see them next week, 'but I suppose Miss Grainger will say she should come?' 'But of course!' said Miss Grainger (educational psychologist) in her slow, calm way. Mrs Willcox and I discussed afterwards how we should manage this visit most easily for the children and staff. Then Miss Beckwith (who will have the family later and who doesn't know them yet) and I went to see the children, playing on the swings. Susan rushed to meet me; I had a less exuberant welcome from Linda and none from Tracey who was doped with a headcold and homesickness.

I told them I'd seen their mother who'd sent her love, and explained again where she is living. Susan told me, 'I don't like this place.' We agreed it isn't like home, but the food and toys are good. I told them I would bring their mother to see them next week, and explained two or three times that she would have to go back to granny's and they would stay here. Inspector Worth had already told them he was going to find another house for them all to live in with their mother. They were full of this and the staff complained later. It is hard to convey the time-lag. Miss Beckwith and I were taken aback to find the children's hair cropped almost to their scalps, because of the head-lice. It seemed unnecessary with the modern treatment available, and I know from experience that drastic hair-cutting is one thing that makes people go quite wild, especially when under any form of restraint. It mightn't have happened if the children hadn't come here on Removal Orders at an unusually low social ebb.

In the car both ways Inspector Worth told me about his work, and the cream (from an interest point of view) of his cases over many years. He recounted about six cases where a housewife was originally 'swimming in filth' and became, with help, 'spotlessly clean'. He hopes Mrs Chubb will react similarly. It's strange how much store older social workers set on cleanliness. Being clean is certainly an effort if one is ill or depressed, so I suppose it's a good indication if not an end in itself, except that increased self-respect causes an upward spiral. A sign of a healthy cow is lick-marks on the coat (and a pig being clean behind the ears) but you don't cure a cow by grooming it, so I suppose it is the relationship (with people) that encourages cleanliness as a by-product rather than repeated exhortations to 'clean the place up'. Mr Worth told me about his colleague in the south Loamshire area, and said he would be willing to help from Marlshire any time.

15 August

Another puncture on the way to work—my tyres are becoming like some of my clothes. From mid-morning onwards I went on a round of far-flung mothers. (At my Loamshire interview, the county children's officer told the committee, 'This is our most far-flung student—in Marlford', which is reminiscent of Rudyard Kipling and made one feel like an outpost of the Barchester empire.) On the way I passed a group of roadmen and recognized Mr Ethel Rock of Long Winkley, who waved back. He must be the only local roadman with the face of a poetic bank-clerk under a trilby hat. I went to the police station in Dencombe to get the rest of the 'Dick Whittington' address of George's mother, Miss Gardiner. I found Miss Gardiner living in a fairly large, detached house—not a bit pleased to see me (not surprisingly, without warning) so I gave her the letter I'd intended to leave if she hadn't been in, and arranged to call back in the afternoon.

Then I went to Withydean, on a road full of mountain ash with red berries. I left a letter at the hotel there for Mrs White, Gregory's mother, asking her to meet me outside at 3.00 p.m., and had a breather beforehand. Mrs White emerged promptly, and we went to a café to talk over a cup of tea. The first time she would only say yes, or 'all right', but she talked about a third of the conversation today and might become quite a chatterbox in time. Apart from having two illegitimate sons, Mrs White lives in an incredible rut. She has lived all her life—thirty-five years—in the same cottage, alone with her husband since she married four years ago. Every Saturday evening her extended family gather together. She has worked in the same hotel for seventeen years, two shifts a day, starting at 7.30 a.m. and finishing at 11.0 p.m. She has had no holiday for three years, and wouldn't go away anyway. She goes to the pictures when her favourite film star is on.

Her husband works irregular hours 'on the timber', so she hardly sees him to speak to, and in any case has no intention of telling him about Gregory. She is still full of her meeting with Gregory and has complete faith in Mrs Victor. She told me quite innocently that she's written to Mrs V but hasn't had a reply yet. Mrs Victor told me she hadn't heard a word. Mrs V (normally) seems as unlikely to tell a lie as George Washington, so she must mind very much. But nobody could be more harmless than Mrs White, with her wish for just an occasional glimpse of Gregory. All I could do was to mention Mrs Victor's fear of losing Gregory to his mother, so that Mrs White won't be too surprised and disappointed if nothing comes of the original meeting. And I advised her to write to Miss Farrar if she wants help in future.

(Miss Farrar thinks I should see Mrs Victor once more and tell her I've seen Mrs White, who says she has written; she agrees I can pretend the letter went astray—which it may have done—but thinks I should add, 'And of course, I know you'll reply when Mrs White writes again.' I don't know that at all, and think it would be best if the Marlford City worker could carry on from here on a slow, long-term basis, but I imagine she has been too dependent on Mrs V for too long.) It's a bit alarming to see how easily you can find yourself ruled by a foster-mother when you need her services so much.

The only solution I can see at the moment is to include the natural parents in the picture from the word go, however remote they seem at that time, and to discuss the child's relationships with his own family when first meeting prospective foster-parents as a vital aspect of the job. It is amazing what foster-parents are willing and able to tackle, and it would save pain later if they could orientate themselves towards this most difficult aspect of their role from the very beginning. On the other hand, it is equally clear, or clearer, that foster-parents grow as close as 'real' parents over a prolonged period of living with the child, so one can't realistically try to work against the grain of these equally 'natural' ties.

Later I went back to Dencombe to see Miss Gardiner. It appeared that she had shaved her upper lip during the afternoon, and generally worked herself into a more receptive state of mind. She is missing her old cottage very much and feels quite out of her depth living in 'this posh house' with her more successful brother. We talked for some time about her son, George. Miss G placed him with Mrs Yates as a baby of 11 weeks old, and says she 'thinks deeply' about having contributed financially for George for thirteen years, while deriving little pleasure herself. Now she is 50, and almost giving up the struggle to be recognized as George's mother. She resents Mrs Yates as being possessive, uneducated and unambitious for George, and yet realizes he has received excellent care in many ways and regards Mr and Mrs Yates as his real parents. Miss Gardiner is hurt by George's attitude, which makes her rude on the rare occasions she does visit him.

George realized he was illegitimate about a year ago, and now has even less opinion of his mother, but is equally critical if she doesn't visit for over a year or fails to send him an Easter egg. Mrs Yates wants me to ensure that Miss G won't suddenly remove George when he leaves school. Miss Gardiner was last visited by a student social worker three years ago. Since then she has nursed both her sister and her father until they died, and was in a low state afterwards, and has recently moved to this new house in the same small town. Now, she told me with shy delight, it is just possible that she is to be married. She didn't enlarge, and I couldn't gather whether it is the sort of country courtship which continues indefinitely. The man doesn't know about George, but she might conceivably ask him if he'd be willing to take on George too. She 'wouldn't push it at all' and, on the whole, she is resigning herself to losing George because she thinks he's at an age to grow away independently anyway.

In fact, Miss Gardiner summed up, she wants to do 'whatever is best for George'. It struck me that she has been very much left out, and I asked whether she'd like further talks with the regular fieldworker. No, she said firmly, she wouldn't—it's too late, and she thinks the last person went straight back and told Mrs Yates all she had said. (Perhaps Mrs Yates gave this impression on purpose.) Miss Gardiner was eager to discuss her position during the interview and then closed it with a business-like snap. She sent her love to George, and will try to visit him soon. So I suppose things will go on much the same.

It's possible that George would regard his mother differently if she became a married woman. Otherwise it's sad to realize that it really is too late if a 13-year-old boy hardly knows his mother, and his foster-parents don't want him to—by this time you have to leave it to his own initiative to some extent. The fostering began on a private basis and the various workers have had differing opinions over the years. Mrs Yates is almost illiterate and primitively maternal, so that she provides a warm but rough and ready home which is frequently criticized by envious neighbours, who seem to feel Mrs Yates attracts unsuitable kudos as a well-known foster-mother.

16 August

Miss Beckwith and I called for Mrs Chubb in Pilbury at 10.00 a.m. to go with her and her 6-year-old son, Dean, to see Linda, Susan and Tracey at Redlands. At 10 a.m. Mrs Chubb came walking along the road to meet us, as smart as she could be—reinforcing my impression of last April that she is very co-operative when she understands what's happening. She sat by me on both journeys and told me various things about her 'plans'. Her separated husband has the new baby son which his cohabitee seemed to be expecting in the spring.

Mrs Chubb went to see her baby, Jayne, in the Marlford City nursery twice last week and told me, in her guileless way, that the baby's condition has improved amazingly in this short time. It is quite foreign to her that she is to be brought to court for treating her children 'in a manner likely'. She sees no need to protest that she's a good mother—because she is, except in material ways. Miss Beckwith coached her towards making further visits to Redlands under her own steam, thus killing two birds, because the report of such an effort would be well received in court later in September, as well as saving our time. Dean sat on Miss Beckwith's knee in the back of the car and chattered incessantly. He has many Chubb characteristics, and is anxious to be a proper part of the family. At first he kept anticipating car crashes, was extremely keen that our car shouldn't be overtaken, and asked a series of questions such as, 'If a little girl stood right in front of the car, what would Mrs Sparrow *do*?' Later he kept telling us how fond he is of Linda, Susan and Tracey, and how 'they are the only kids in the world'.

We met Mrs Willcox at Redlands, and went into the garden to find the children. It was a quiet meeting, and we left Mrs Chubb with her four children clustered round her for nearly an hour. Miss Beckwith and I talked in the office with Mrs Willcox. The little girls seem to be getting their usual enjoyment out of Redlands but have reached 'a grizzly stage' and Mrs W is relieved they are tall enough only to pull each other's ears. Sleeping arrangements have been adapted to suit the children who are not used to a hygienic one to a bed, but accustomed to eight in two beds in one room (Mrs C + three men + themselves and the baby) or eight in a car. Tracey, nearly 3 years old, is particularly missing her mother and needs continual nursing, which she has developed to a fine art. It is typical of Susan that she came to see me during her mother's visit—her sisters were engrossed.

The Redlands staff didn't want Mrs Chubb to visit again before 31 August, and were on pins about the immediate parting. I wasn't apprehensive to the same extent although it was most unpleasant when it happened. (It is comforting at the cinema to realize that the man who is wandering alone in a dark house can't himself hear the accompanying music which reaches a climax of suspense and makes it inevitable that the man shall be coshed by a hidden enemy. The prolonged, apprehensive music is almost worse to bear than being hit on the head, which is real and quickly over. Even so, the suspense music is possibly meant to represent the victim's feelings, in which case he is spared nothing in advance.)

At noon I went into the garden followed by some of the staff, to separate the family which was huddled together in a clinging mass. They all knew it was going to happen and it happened quickly with an uproar of noisy crying. Mrs Chubb and Dean did their utmost, waving and calling from the car that they would come again soon. The staff saw us off, standing in a row with set, unhappy faces, holding Linda and Susan's hands, with Tracey struggling frantically in their arms. Mrs Chubb was quiet on the return journey and Dean went thankfully to sleep on her knee. She imagined her daughters would settle again quite soon, and knew instinctively that this way is better than not visiting at all. I said goodbye to her in Pilbury, and Miss Beckwith arranged to visit her next week.

In the late afternoon I went for the last time to the Hicks family in Andersham who have Carmen placed for adoption, now $4\frac{1}{2}$ months old. They were out but turned up all together eventually at Carmen's bedtime. Mrs Hicks sat with me and Carmen in the living-room, feeding her and getting her ready for bed. Mr Hicks took care of everything else—bringing Carmen's night-clothes, her bottle, making a meal for Leslie (aged 10) and a cup of tea for me. Then he and Leslie came and sat down with us. Carmen is very interested in faces, and they are endlessly pleased to entertain her. Leslie particularly amuses himself and her by making a series of funny faces at her which are actually semi-aggressive, which I suppose is quite good for him. It reminded me of teasing generally which can be welcomed as a sign of affection or resented because of the underlying hostility. Both types of teasing take much the same form outwardly to an impartial observer, but the parties concerned usually know perfectly well what's underneath, even if unwittingly, and react accordingly.

This was an ordinary final interview. The Hicks still haven't received the mother's consent, but everything is set for when they do have it and, unless I were to turn up again bearing the consent form actually in my hand, there seems little further support one can give here. Mrs Merrill of the Marlford Adoption Society will stay in touch until the court hearing, though the three months' welfare supervision period is almost complete. Whether or not Carmen is finally adopted by this family (surely she will be) is one of the things I must know after leaving. This is the sort of thing which would tend to prevent my leaving a future job because you never reach a stage where everything in the gardens of all your cases is lovely, having achieved a simultaneously natural conclusion. As one could never hope to have a final harvesting any more than one can in farming, the least one can do is to stay long enough in one job to be more than a brief disturbing influence.

17 August

A.m. in the office. In the afternoon 'discussed' with Miss Farrar her final report on my placement here. She is sorry the Barchester University regulations prevent my reading it, but I was a bit taken aback to hear as much as I did. The main criticism seems to be that I'm 'sometimes rather slow', which is disquieting when I shall soon be employed with a full workload, but I suppose one is bound to seem slow off the mark when passively resisting some of my superiors' aims for situations known to me at first hand, instead of telling them straight when I'd prefer to do things a little differently.

In the late afternoon I went to Rickerton—first to see Yvonne who has recently arrived from East Dowling to her new foster-home with her great-aunt, Mrs Nash. The situation, so nebulous earlier, became real to me as soon as I recognized Yvonne (aged 13) in the road as a potential trouble-spot, even before discovering who she was. I happened to arrive during a gathering of the peculiar family clans, and so met Yvonne's brother who is with their mother, who is living in a caravan in Marlshire with another man. They were all friendly, and Yvonne is settling well so far. Mrs Nash asked me for a bicycle from the committee, and the mother (with a face a bit like Miss Murphy's—sophisticated and rather hard) asked for help in getting a council house, determined not to be outdone. Mrs Nash is delighted with Yvonne but I think is glad now to be a protected foster-mother as well as great-aunt. Yvonne seems almost unable to contain whatever underlies her extremely superficial friendliness. I'm visiting once more next week to introduce Miss Beckwith; also the Hopgood family, whom she will continue to visit.

Today outside the Hopgoods' front door I could hear: the radio blaring, a child crying, Mr Hopgood growling, Mrs Hopgood snapping, and frying fat sizzling. Mrs H opened the door, looking demure as usual. It's been 'a happy week', and she is still having an orgy of redecorating so we stood in the bare living-room while she recited the events of her week. Then I called at the Brayley Children's Home to say goodbye to Mr and Mrs Coombs, whom I like very much. They have just got a student from a residential child care course with whom I compared notes. It turned out that the student is seconded from Loamshire for the course, and will return there after Christmas so we're likely to meet again later.

18 August

Memorable because I had the last interview with my bête noire et blanche—Mrs Almond of Drayton. It's obvious that the recent crisis has had repercussions on Mrs A's physical health, and I started by asking how she was. She says she's recovering, but 'I've been feeling—not guilty exactly' (a big admission) ... 'but as though I've been under great strain.' It took one and a half hours for her to tell me 'the whole story' (nutshell on pp. 127–8).

It all started when Miss Murphy 'interfered' in her sister's marriage and the husband Dick went wild, locked both women up and threatened to murder Miss Murphy and her younger son, Shaun. Next day the women and child sought refuge with Mrs Almond. 'And there was I,' said Mrs A, 'stuck like a flipping lemon'—for ten days. Gradually she realized, from overhearing quarrels, that Miss Murphy was trying to prevent her sister from returning to Dick the husband, and that Miss M was working towards taking a flat for just her sister, herself, and her two sons, Eamon and Shaun. Once settled there she would perhaps have made her sister responsible for the two boys and been considerably more independent herself. To avoid this, Mrs Almond 'brought husband and wife together', and turned Miss Murphy out.

Although she sees Shaun as 'a devil', it seems that Mrs A is most uncomfortable about having turned a child out of her own house, which has revolved round many children. Apparently Miss Murphy (when she was angry with her sister for going back to the latter's husband) made a casual reference to leaving Shaun with Mrs Almond, who had replied, 'Oh no, you don't! You're not going to treat your sister as you've treated me! She's brought that child up, and you're not going to take him away from her.' I think Mrs Almond has tried to insure herself in several ways:

(a) She has actively helped Miss M's sister, and feels that this sister is now less likely to hurt her back by harbouring Eamon in future.

(b) She recognizes a fellow-sufferer in Miss M's sister and made sure she retained Shaun, so Fate is more likely to let her (Mrs A) keep Eamon.

(c) She encouraged Miss M's sister to claim payment for keeping Shaun. This means both that there is no advantage to Miss Murphy in moving Eamon to her sister's if she has to pay double or, if she didn't pay at all, her sister couldn't afford to keep two boys.

Mrs Almond doesn't voice (a) (b) (c) of course, but I think from my own dealings with her that this is how her mind works!

All this leaves Miss Murphy in rather a pitiful position. It is now quite clear that she has no intention of looking after the two boys by herself. She talks of this in her wilder moments but would find it difficult to carry out consistent care. She is still half enjoying herself in adolescent style so unless she marries eventually and settles down, she wouldn't want her freedom curtailed by two boys. She seems half ashamed of her sons and half determined to stay near them, tending to use them as weapons or presents in withholding or giving them to the people towards whom she is ambivalent. Therefore her apparent choices now are:

(1) To leave things as they are. After a crisis, Miss M soon behaves 'as though nothing had happened'. She has an extraordinary tie with Mrs Almond which I can't visualize ever snapping completely.

(2) To find another private foster-home for Eamon. This would be difficult and Eamon would be unco-operative. She would still have to pay, so the only advantage would be in spiting Mrs A.

(3) To absorb Eamon into her sister's household, which is what

she wanted to do, I think, but Mrs A forestalled this, apparently on a more certain basis.

Of course Miss Murphy is the last person to sit down and think (1) (2) (3). She isn't an easy person to 'help' and has a long-standing resentment towards 'welfare'. Recently I think she has found Mrs Almond stronger than she bargained for, which may be a roundabout relief. I imagine Miss M is infuriated by Mrs A's frequent self-righteous homilies. But Mrs A has been more natural and human in her recent dealings with Miss M, and perhaps the latter would appreciate this even if it was unpleasant at the time. Instead of her usual grieved, holier-than-thou approach, Mrs Almond herself recognizes that she has been openly 'nasty to Miss M on her own level'—for example, 'I've known you twelve years too long.' It may be wishful thinking to hope this might have cleared débris masking the positive feeling between them.

As for Eamon, Mrs Almond says 'he's a different boy' (which she's said at least twice before)—happier and freer. He is 'more thoughtful' to Mrs A, and it is openly acknowledged that his mother is important to him even though he feels it safer to stay with Mrs A. Eamon has met his mother outside since the upheaval, and I expect she may soon start visiting him at home again, as Mrs A doesn't intend to stop her. I was glad to hear that Eamon has just started going every morning to the local people who originally took him to the RC church and who taught him the catechism. He had 'stayed away from them for months' but now has a regular morning job of caring for some puppies there. So it looks as though, having broken Father O'Sullivan's windows, he can now bear to renew a former RC contact, even if only on a puppy level.

It becomes steadily more obvious that his attitude to RCism is bound up with Miss M and Mrs A and the conflicting pressures they put on him. Mrs A seems to have dealt with the broken windows in a business-like way, and is not going to taunt Miss M with the bill. She seemed relieved when I said this incident seemed healthier than his nightmares of the spring term. She heartily agreed, and was able to mention for the first time that Eamon had played truant once or twice in the summer term. She volunteered that she will have 'to handle Eamon firmly and gently' if we are to avoid his becoming delinquent. She thinks the next six months will see her over the worst. Sometimes she wonders if she can continue under the strain, 'but as I've gone on so long, I can manage this last little bit to finish the job—I'm a stubborn person you know.'

When the story was over, I was uncomfortable that there is so little one can say or do, and that I'd have to say goodbye to Mrs Almond this time, which she seemed to have forgotten. I did suggest her having a holiday. . . . Mrs A of course doesn't really change but she did seem a bit different today. It is as if she was forced recently by events either to become more human or to crack altogether. She looks tired and older, but the barrier of sickly artificiality seemed less apparent today. Her trite, senti-mental phrases have had a horrid fascination for me. In contrast today it was refreshing to hear her say things like 'There was I, stuck like a flipping lemon.' She was near tears a lot of the time and also laughed aloud several times—both new in my experience of her. She was more open about feelings of guilt, nastiness and anger than I've heard before. Previous upsets seemed to heighten the off-key holiness; today she seemed less sugary, more robust and approachable. She still wishes the government would think up some clause to protect people like Eamon (and herself).

All this is making the best of a bad job, because towards the end my toes were curling up through apprehension about the em-barrassingly emotional parting she might inflict. I gave her Mrs Garvey's card for future reference because she cannot remember our names, and left a message for Eamon who was out swimming. In an effort to ease our goodbyes, I said I'd be interested in further news (meaning through the department)—she said she'd like to write to me, and even suggested bringing Eamon over to south Loamshire for an occasional day trip. I'm not sure how far she meant this, and think it will fade out naturally, but it took me aback, and I made a vague reply. At the door she called me Pet twice without apologizing, and I nearly lost my hand. Finally she said, 'God bless!' I could only reply, 'The same to you!' and took the rest of the afternoon very gently (paddling in a river on the way back to Marlford).

19 August

In the office—I spent a long time writing pages about the above situation in compensation because really all I can do with Mrs Almond is listen, and think and write it down.

It occurred to me long after Miss Farrar's surprising idea (on the morning of 15 June) that I should get Eamon back to the RC church before I left, that she perhaps only meant this if Father O'Sullivan wouldn't agree to a breather—i.e. she was assuming he wouldn't agree whereas I was assuming he would. It turned out afterwards that nobody except myself imagined he could agree—I thought he was bound to accept such a reasonable request! So it was just as well I visited him in simple faith without being disillusioned beforehand.

Also I went through George Gardiner's files and did a social history for him.

22 August

I spent the day in south Loamshire (a week before starting work there) being introduced to families that my fellow Barchester student knows before she leaves. I met other colleagues in the morning and read records, and nipped round eight families with the student-worker in the afternoon, and then will pick up about sixteen more situations to start off with. I transferred my 'oak tree' from the Marlford office to the south Loamshire office, where it was happily received. The acorn was planted in December, sprouted in March about the time the placement began, and is now about a foot tall and flourishing. The symbolic weeds which grew simultaneously were past their prime and had green-fly, so were removed today.

I dreamt about the Mrs Almond-Miss Murphy situation, and am not sure whether this made it better or worse.

23 August

After much thought I composed a letter to Eamon's mother, Miss Murphy—and was surprised later to find that Miss Farrar thought it should be more non-committal 'because it's really a case of least said soonest mended with her', and one can't know how she'd take any letter without knowing her immediate mood that morning. So I was pleased to write another instead—just saying I'm 'sorry' not to see her again; that Mrs Garvey will continue to visit Eamon occasionally and will be willing to get in touch with Miss Murphy any time the latter wishes.

East Dowling continues to write about Yvonne settling down with her great-aunt-foster-mother Mrs Nash, and we are still clarifying our roles with regard to Yvonne—which committee shall make which decisions, and how payments shall be made.

The German authorities want more news of Erika. Unfortunately Miss Onslow (child guidance clinic) is on holiday, because I should have liked a reason for hearing about her early impressions of the Strickland family. As it is, I'm writing both to our opposite numbers in Germany and to Miss Onslow, suggesting that they get in direct touch in future.

The Marlford City children's officer wrote about the Chubb family. Apparently when Mrs Chubb first visited their nursery to see Jayne, Matron gave her a baby boy half Jayne's age by mistake. It wasn't until Mrs Chubb remarked how much 'Jayne' had grown in less than a week that Matron realized what had happened. They think it distinctly odd that Mrs Chubb shouldn't recognize her own baby although everyone is pleased by the improvement in Jayne's health. I replied giving details about arrangements for the court case, mentioning how dim Mrs Chubb is in some ways, and refraining from pointing out that the incident may be more indicative of Matron's incompetence than of Mrs Chubb's.

About lunchtime I called on Mrs Victor and spoke with her on the doorstep for a few minutes, ostensibly to see whether she is travelling to Barchester with me on Friday when I leave—unfortunately she can't now, as the person who is standing in for her isn't available until Saturday. I told her I'd seen Mrs White last week, who'd mentioned that she had written to thank Mrs Victor—'so the letter may have gone astray in the post. . . .' Mrs V looked rather sad, said nothing and changed the subject, leaving me with the uncomfortable impression that she knew that I knew. . . . We talked generally a little longer and then said goodbye finally.

I've enjoyed meeting Mrs Victor and her six lively foster-children, and hearing about their rich life together as well as her previous careers. But she might almost come into the category of semi-hostile client—it takes me a longish time to spot them. For one thing she prefers always to know best, and then the idea of Gregory and Joe's mothers has really been too much for her. She seemed to enjoy portraying the foster-home, particularly perhaps in order to keep off more dangerous topics. Most people were ordinarily interested, if and when I told them I was a student, temporarily in Marlshire—but Mrs Victor just nodded graciously as though I'd confessed something only too apparent which she was trying to overlook.

In the afternoon I went to the other two 'basic foster-homes' in Drayton for the last time. Mrs Yates talked for one and a half hours while I was nearly hypnotized by her barely intelligible Marlshire brogue plus stammer. Jimmy and George kept popping in, but she pushed them out to do errands and was determined to get full value in this last interview. She had thought up several topics over which she or her neighbours needed help and advice. She hoped George's mother, Miss Gardiner, had been polite to me because she's inclined to be 'rude and jealous'. I didn't say much about Miss G, except that she hopes to visit soon, and Mrs Yates began to point out some of Miss G's nicer qualities.

Mrs Yates is thrilled that George has come second in his D stream form at school, and wants me to tell Mr Tasker that 'George is ready to take his exams', although she has no idea what sort of exams they are. She was amusing on the subject of her recent interview with Jimmy's ex-headmistress about Jimmy going to the special school (18 July). Beforehand the head told us that she feared she wouldn't be able to persuade Mrs Yates to agree to special education, so asked us to do it. But Mrs Yates sounded as though she'd had to persuade the head to agree, and had had to explain carefully that his old school is unable to give Jimmy the 'special little lift' he needs, because the staff and form-master were so reluctant to lose him. Before I left, both boys were ushered forward to shake hands.

Recently it's been difficult to find Sally's foster-mother, Mrs Bateson, at home, but as this afternoon was almost the last chance I waited outside in my car for one and a half hours, being entertained by the 4-year-old boy from next door who was desperately wanting to play with Sally, and perhaps hoping I would smuggle him in with me if he looked after me meanwhile. By the time Mr Bateson cycled up at 5.00 p.m. I'd almost forgotten why I'd come, and made the mistake of calling him by Sally's surname. Later I saw Mrs Bateson, Sally and David for a few minutes before saying goodbye. I think this has been the only plain-sailing family —or apparently on an even keel at present. I should have told the people I don't see very often in advance that I was leaving. They

143

were all told at the beginning and it didn't occur to me that they might forget in between.

24 August

A.m. worked in the office; had a final supervision session with Miss Farrar. She says she's usually sorry to see students leave because she doesn't fully know what they're facing in the next stage, but she isn't sorry in this case because I'm half-settled in Loamshire already.

Later in the afternoon Miss Beckwith and I went to Rickerton. First we had a cup of tea and a longish talk with Mrs Nash and Yvonne. It's nice to see that Mrs Nash looks like being a foster-mother who really values a fieldworker's support as I imagine she will need this sooner or later.

Then we went to the Hopgoods, and found Mrs H, Keith and Sam and Karen all barefoot and the house in chaos. The health visitor had called, and criticized the state of the garden, so Mrs H has tackled that too, and showed us the blister it caused her. She was looking for sympathy the whole time today, especially over her stomach pains. She is afraid it may mean an operation and she's sure she wouldn't wake up from the anaesthetic. According to a book I've read recently, this fear may have something to do with her sleeplessness. Keith and Sam were a little more friendly today in showing us their water-pistols. The three children look well in spite of their scruffiness. Mrs H told Miss Beckwith, with the dignity she produces on these occasions, that she will 'be pleased to go on being visited'.

This turned out to be my last visit of all, and I'm sorry to lose Mrs Hopgood.

25 August

Mostly in the office. 10.00 a.m. final discussion with Mr Tasker for nearly one and a half hours. We went through the Eamon Murphy case again from where we last talked about it after I saw Father O'Sullivan. He wants to edit it for use as case material because it's 'pioneer work on a child protection case, which usually is hardly touched'. Fortunately or unfortunately at the beginning I'd no idea what thin ice I was on in attempting to move a private foster-child swiftly from one church to another.

This morning I knew I'd be expected to criticize the arrangements for practical training of students in Marlshire, but didn't think it worth racking my brains over because, as I told him, they have developed it to a fine art by now. I could only think that, if I were here for longer, I might find the policy on receptions into care a bit worrying—although, with experience, one would investigate the family situation thoroughly before having to argue about it in the office. It does seem odd that policy isn't more uniform throughout the country instead of being dependent, as Mr Tasker says, on whether a local authority is making a drive towards spectacular public care or a maxim of private care, and upon the unconscious motivations of senior staff who may or may not want children to stay in their own homes.

During the afternoon I finished all records, dictated final letters plus a few memos to fieldstaff, saw about medical cards and school reports, went to see the county treasurer about an interim cheque for Mrs Nash, wrote CHA forms returning ten children borrowed from (or added to) Mrs Garvey and Miss Beckwith's caseloads, cleared out the desk drawers and seem to have finished. Two fellow students, or their supervisors, telephoned from Loamshire to ask for a lift back to Barchester tomorrow, as one has had a slight car accident and the other's car is exhausted.

26 August

An odd day—I asked Miss Beckwith if there was anything I could do for her, as she seems to have the most hectic time of the fieldworkers, and she wanted me to do social histories, which she hasn't time for, for three of her foster-children—so it was a case of beginning on entirely new files and often it felt more like a first day than a last. These three children are part of a family of eleven and—but there's no point in enlarging now.

Everybody was very pleasant in saying goodbye, with the general feeling that there's no need to because I shan't be far off and can drop into the Marlford office in future. I must have been mad to have a preconceived idea that there was an almost indefinable namby-pamby element in field social work. In fact it's been far more enjoyable, satisfying and stimulating than I'd hoped, with wide enough scope to include all sorts of interests which one wouldn't expect to come together in one whole job.

Even this log-book has come to an end without being organized, as exactly as if it had been tailor-made—so my last impression is that things have fitted with a sense of rightness, except that there are still plenty of future developments I'd like to know about people I've met in Marlshire, which is just like farming—you have to start ploughing again straight after harvest, even before thatching.

Postscript

Next evening at a party half sadly celebrating the end of the course, another student told me of a snippet of conversation she had recently overheard between the south Loamshire area officer and the county children's officer: 'Jane Sparrow must trust us already because she's brought her oak tree. . . .' 'Brought her what?' he asked.

Carried away through celebrating, I said something on these lines to fellow students, 'Yes, and I shall keep that oak tree for the rest of my career, and on the day of my retirement it will be enormous, and there'll be a procession through the streets bearing the oak tree with me sitting aloft, and the town band's trumpets will be playing full blast. . . .' My tutor in turn overheard this embarrassing piece of conceited nonsense, and simply said, 'Have some more beer, Jane?' I rapidly came down to earth, but was glad at last to realize there was no need any more to watch my words, having been unduly careful for far too long, after five years' previous employment at Downcroft.

It only remains to say that I was soon settled in Loamshire for the best part of a decade with most enjoyable colleagues. The oak tree, as things turned out, did not last as well as I did, but perhaps my roots took over where its left off, as it was no longer a necessary symbol once it had survived two or three years. What was so good about Loamshire, in contrast with Downcroft, was that we were able to work positively for the children in our care and with the many families we knew closely in our area. As I have never subsequently kept a diary, except for daily appointments and mileage records, there will be nothing further to write in quite this form again.